The Attitude of the Masters

Céline Théron

Foreword by Rene Godefroy

An Imprint of InQuest Publishing

The Attitude of the Masters

By Céline Théron

Copyright © 2014, Céline Théron

All rights reserved. Printed and bound in the United States of America. No part of this book may be reproduced or transmitted in any manner whatsoever without written permission except in the case of brief quotations embodied in critical articles and reviews.

For more information, contact
InQuest Publishing:
3589 Mill Creek Trail
Smyrna, GA 30082

Printed in the United States of America
Printed on acid-free, recycled paper

ISBN: 978-0-9719754-2-2

Dedication

In memory of my mother,
Zizabai Théron

Contents

Acknowledgements... vii

Foreword by Rene Godefroy... ix

Introduction... xi

The Buddha Attitude.. 1

Do Not Fight With Darkness.. 25

Your Intimate Enemy Is Fear.. 33

Your Faithful Servant... 49

You Are The Positive Force.. 65

There Is Wisdom In Your Suffering.................................... 75

Persist Until You Succeed... 91

The Laws Of Nature... 107

Journey Into Your Inner World.. 121

Sharing Makes The World Better...................................... 131

Epilogue... 144

Resources... 145

ACKNOWLEDGEMENTS

I want to pause for a moment to express a deep sense of gratitude to Rene Godefroy for encouraging me to write this book. Rene, without you, this book would not be possible. In spite of your busy schedule, you found the time to coach, mentor, and guide me. You are such a patient and kind teacher.

I am deeply touched by your generosity. Words are not enough to fully express how I feel about the way you bring the best out of me. After every coaching session with you, I experience a new awakening.

You often say, "Life is like a book. We can either study it or let it gather dust on the shelves of the world." Well, you inspire me to study mine. Thank you for being such a blessing.

I wish to thank my father, Albert Théron, a French Army veteran who served in war. I still remember you as the man with a giant heart who was willing to help whoever came your way. I was deeply touched and inspired by your altruism.

I also wish to thank my mother, Zizabai Théron. *Amma*, you were the essence of my life. Your inspiration created a profound transformation in me. You are still living in my heart. The thought of you fills my heart with deepest love and gratitude. Words are not enough to express those feelings. I will never forget that your lips were always singing the name

The Attitude of the Masters *by Céline Théron*

of the Lord. You would often say, "Céline, thank God each and every day at dawn." Every day, I thank God for being blessed to have had you as my mother.

A special thanks to my eldest sister, Claudine Théron, for taking such great care of me in my early years. You supported me fully in my study. You had the courage to step up and assume the burden of taking care of the whole family even at a young age. I am very grateful to you.

My thanks to my sister, Jeanine Selva, for your gentle spirit and your attention in making sure I ate delicious dishes. You were never tired of preparing and serving us good foods. I am grateful to you.

I also express thanks to my sister Aline Théron. Aline, although you were a child just like me, you held my hand to make sure we got to school safe and together. Since then, you have been on my side during my journey. You have always been there for me during my trials and tribulations. I am grateful for your caring.

Finally, I wish to thank my nephew and niece, Albert and Victoria. You are such beautiful children. Your love, smiles and sweet words always give me joy.

FOREWORD

As a devout student of personal development books and the author of three of them, I am delighted to write the foreword for *The Attitude Of The Masters*. As you might know, we are living in very uncertain times. Every day we wake up to deal with a chaotic world. Most people are beaten and discouraged. This world is changing at an alarming rate. Therefore, we need a lot of motivation and inspiration. This book is definitely much needed.

Celine Theron and I never met in person. We met each other over the Internet. When she approached me for coaching, I wasn't sure I would be able to take on another client. My schedule was extremely busy. But after a few email exchanges, I decided to bring her on board. Well, I'm so glad I did. I discovered a wise and deeply passionate difference maker in Celine. Yes, I coached and mentored her. However, she became my coach as well. I have learned so much from her insights.

Between the pages of this book, you will discover some profound and life-transforming lessons to create the life you want. Celine shares the simple ways you can use your mind to become a powerful person. In *The Attitude Of The Masters*, you will learn how to proactively create the life you want instead of reacting to events and circumstances.

What really excite me about Celine Theron's book is how

The Attitude of the Masters *by Céline Théron*

she is able to dive deep into her Indian culture to surface with pearls of wisdom that are relevant to us all. Of course many author's talk about wisdom from the Far East. But, very few of them actually lived and experienced what they write or talk about. They'd rather share what they learned from books or heard from others. On the contrary, Celine is deeply entrenched into Eastern culture. She speaks with authority on the subject.

At first, I thought Celine chose me to write the foreword because of my credibility and celebrity status in the field of personal development. After all, I'm the bestselling author of the book *Kick Your Excuses Goodbye*. But, I was wrong. I discovered that Celine chose me because I exemplify the attitude of the masters. Thanks to this book and the insights I learned from Celine.

I don't know what you are going through in your life. But, here's what I know: You are either dealing with a problem, finishing dealing with one, or you are heading toward one. That's just life. Whatever it is for you, this book is definitely the one book that will empower you to face your challenges with courage and determination.

I travel all over North America to deliver motivational speeches at corporations and associations. People from all walks of life approach me to share their stories of struggles with me. They are looking for new ways and fresh insights to deal with their problems. This book, without a doubt, gives lots of fresh ideas to deal with new challenges.

I highly recommend you read every page of *The Attitude Of The Masters*. In fact, you should read it a second time. Take lots of notes. Tell all of your friends and family members about it.

Rene Godefroy
Motivational Keynote Speaker
Bestselling author of *Kick Your Excuses Goodbye*

INTRODUCTION

Over the years, many people have asked me questions about Indian customs and traditions. They are often curious about the red dot on my forehead. They want to know its meaning. Well, we call it *pottu*. It is also known as *kumkum, tilakam,* or *bindi.* It seems as though my exotic and mystical homeland fascinates many people. My main goal in this book is to give you a glance at some ancient Indian traditions, and the wisdom of its masters.

Please understand that I am sharing my personal views with you. They are the lenses through which I see and observe the world. I believe what makes a person different from others is his or her attitude. No, I do not have all the answers. Just like you, I'm searching for answers to the riddles of life.

We all desire to have success. I'm not sure what success means and looks like to you. For most people in Western society, it is defined as gaining material things and external recognition. It is all about having more. What so many people fail to grasp is that the essence of success is to *be* more. The *Vedanta* (a Hindu philosophy) tells us that the greatness of a person is not measured by what he does or has, but by what he *is*. The ultimate growth of human beings is to unfold the divinity inside them.

Simply put, true and lasting success lies in your attitude toward growing and becoming more. Our greatest masters

The Attitude of the Masters *by Céline Théron*

in India set out to be successful human beings first. Then, achievement and wealth followed them because of who they came to be. In this book, you will come to discover *The Attitude of the Masters*. When you embrace their attitude, you will know true joy. You will also begin to experience a meaningful, fulfilling, and enlightened life.

My hope is that you will become more aware that you are essentially a spiritual being living on earth. Reading this book is an opportunity to begin looking at the world in a different way and to have a more enriching life as a result.

Céline Théron

CHAPTER ONE
The Buddha Attitude

The Buddha Attitude

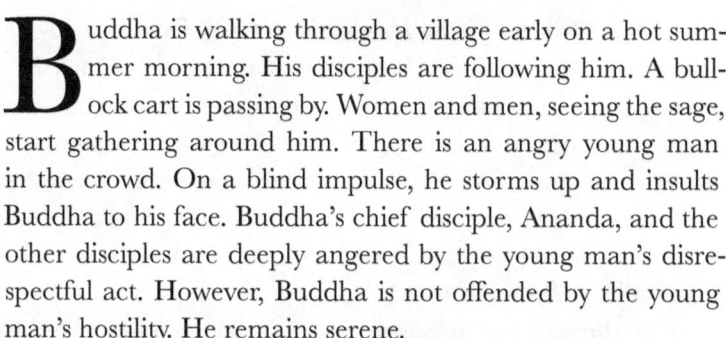

Buddha is walking through a village early on a hot summer morning. His disciples are following him. A bullock cart is passing by. Women and men, seeing the sage, start gathering around him. There is an angry young man in the crowd. On a blind impulse, he storms up and insults Buddha to his face. Buddha's chief disciple, Ananda, and the other disciples are deeply angered by the young man's disrespectful act. However, Buddha is not offended by the young man's hostility. He remains serene.

He simply asks, "Tell me. What would happen if you bought a gift for someone, and that person refused to accept the gift? Who would the gift belong to then?"

The man is surprised at this unexpected question. "As I bought the gift, it would belong to me." He replies.

"In the same way, since I do not accept your insults, they remain with you." Buddha replies in turn.

Buddha's words left a perplexed look on the young man's face.

The day after, Buddha is sitting silently near the bank of a river. The young man halts before Buddha with a disturbed expression on his face. His eyes are clouded by tears. He throws himself at Buddha's feet. The man says, "Oh! Great Master, forgive me for what I did yesterday."

With great compassion, Buddha says, "But I am not the same man to whom you did it." He gestures towards the river flowing by and says, "The Ganges goes on flowing. It is never the same Ganges again. Every man is a river too. You also are not the same man that you were yesterday. You were angry yesterday, but today you touch my feet. So let us forget about forgiveness. You did not hurt me."

Buddha had the attitude of the master. He was not moved by the respect and insult or the praise and blame of other people. Buddha was a master of himself. The greatest challenge you will ever face in your life is becoming a master of yourself.

Have the Attitude of the Master in All You Do

Ask yourself if you have the attitude of the master. One can't keep a dog in order to be called a master. He has to overcome many challenges to become a master. The path to becoming a master is arduous. Wherever he is, and whatever he does, the master remains a master. You can tie his hands and feet and throw him in the sea, but he will come up to the surface with a beautiful pearl in his hand.

Gandhi was put in prison. But, no one could enslave his ideals. Although in prison, he remained a master, not a prisoner or a slave. He was free. The master is free like the birds in the sky.

You are a master, not a slave. Do whatever you do as a master, whether you study, work, or relax. When you do something of your own free will because you want to do it and enjoy doing it, you have the attitude of the master. Conversely, when you do something because you feel forced to do it, or you do not have the strength to control it, you do not act as a master. This is especially true about people's attitudes about going to work.

The Buddha Attitude

Work to Live or Live to Work

People have two extreme attitudes about work. Many go to the workplace without joy. They see it is as a punishment, whereas others act as if they are born to work.

Work fulfills the basic need to be fed. Food is vital. However, man needs more than food; only animals live to eat. People want a good standard of living. Some people give all their energy, time, brain power, and body to achieving a high standard of living. But once they achieve their goals, they have no time left to enjoy life.

Work is necessary to earn a living. And what does living mean? Life is meant to be fully lived in its entire dimension, not according to just one element of it.

Today, many people simply live to work. Every element of their daily lives gets transformed into something work-related to the point the space between home and office disappears. At the end of their working day, they go back home with their office files or carry their office in their mind. Once at home, they talk about work. They do not have time to spend with their children or spouse. They miss the happiness of sharing with their loved ones. They do not know the joy of life.

Obsession with work makes people forget about the higher significance of life. Work gives us money to provide a good standard of living. Unfortunately, work has become an end rather than a means to an end for many of us. Life is meant for play, laughter, and celebration.

You are the master of your life. Your activity is under your control. No oppressor can make you his slave without your cooperation. You become a slave to your work of your own accord. Working all day is not enough. You continue working even at night. The time you should be spending sleeping is considered a waste of productive time.

Socrates warned, "Beware of the barrenness of the busy life." So ask yourself this: "Do I work to live or live to work?"

The Attitude of the Masters *by Céline Théron*

Slow Down so You Can Achieve more

Most people are too busy *doing* something. But all your activities are not necessary for your success. Slowing down the tempo of your daily life would be a good thing for you to do.

But slowing down is almost impossible for someone who is in a rat race. You know better than anybody else that if you slow down, you will lose the race. If you pause even for a few minutes, your competitor will overtake you. The real problem, however, is that you are in a race with no end. Once you have achieved your goal, what's next? You have certainly planned another goal. You have new projects to achieve or ideas to realize. There is no end. Slowing down has become hard because people are conditioned to achieve something. If not, life is purposeless for them. The attitude of the achiever is always to look for new peaks. He is restless. He is no longer living in the present. For him, the present is merely preparation for the future.

Desire motivates a person to achieve. To become successful, you need a burning desire to make it happen. However, the nature of desire is endless. Rare is the heart that will say, "That is enough! I have everything!" However, desire loses its charm once the object you want is in your hands.

The most beautiful, desirable woman would become less of an attraction once she became your wife. You have an ambition to buy a new car. Once you get it, you would want a bigger one. Desire leads you into many vicious circles. Once you acquire something you desire you then find it is not enough and that you crave something else.

You eventually accumulate so many desires, so many horizons, and so many goals to be reached, that you can't slow down. One life is not enough to achieve all you want. So you are in a hurry because your time is limited.

Think about what is essential in your life. The essential is never more and more things, but a main goal. When you know what your main goal is, you do not have to go from one activity to another.

The Buddha Attitude

Adopt the attitude of the masters toward work: slow down! The masters know the art of achieving fast by slowing down. Slowing down is about sitting down and calmly thinking through all your activities to discover which ones are critical to your success. That is how you achieve more with less. That is how you can eliminate stress. That is how you boost productivity. The question you should ask yourself is this: "Is what I'm doing now absolutely critical to my success? If I stop what I'm doing now, can I still achieve the results I am after?"

If you can slow down, sit quietly, and think through what you are doing, you can discover which things in your daily routine are unnecessary. The minute you get rid of what is unnecessary, what remains are the vital few actions that are critical to your success.

Slowing down brings you tranquility. Tranquility is essential for success and fulfillment in any walk of life. Your calm, unstressed attitude is the source of energy, creativity, and self-confidence. It is as important for a mystic as it is for a businessman, a scientist, an artist, an engineer, or a workman. By slowing down, you can achieve more. The calmer we are, the better we work, the greater the amount of work we can do. When you are calm, you bring the greatest quality to your work. It is only when the mind is very calm and collected that the whole of its energy is spent doing good work. Life is meant to be lived fully. If you slow down, you can live, work, and feel well.

Conquer Yourself First and You Will Win

Near a silent river, a frog is eating worms. The snake with its frightening hissing approaches the frog, seizes its prey, and swallows it. The *garuda* (eagle) in the air is circling and gazing hungrily upon the snake. It grasps the snake with its sharp claws and soars into the sky. One animal dominates another.

There will be something that can dominate you. You will always find someone who has something more than you. He might be more talented, more handsome, more clever, happier, stronger or kinder. If you live your life on a basis of

The Attitude of the Masters *by Céline Théron*

comparison, then you will live in a constant state of struggle to have more than others.

Do not think that having more than others is always the way to be the winner. A flexible squirrel can reach the top of the tree but the wild lion can just look at the top from the base of the tree. A feeble thing is strong too. A straw floating on the water can save a drowning man.

Society teaches us to be a winner. In this process, you try to excel beyond all human limitations. People want to be winners because, deep down, they want to "be somebody." We have a faulty idea that we have to be at the top of the mountain or reach the moon to be somebody. But you are a unique person in your own way, so you do not need to prove your uniqueness to anyone.

When a jar is being half-filled with water, it makes a noise. But, when it is full, there is no noise. The masters are like the full jar. They don't make noise to prove that they are somebody. Neil Armstrong, the man who first walked on the moon, loved his farm. He was a humble person who shied away from an adoring public. When the winner bows, all things are elated. When he has a humble attitude, living creatures rejoice.

In our desire to become a winner, some people search for short cuts. People will whisper that, if you are honest, you cannot win. There are times when someone is determined to climb the ladder of success in their company. He fights for it. He does whatever is necessary, including mistreating others. Once he reaches the top of the ladder, he realizes that he does not want to be there. He is unhappy. He lives with regrets.

Choose the attitude of a real winner. They have become successful by hard work, smart use of their talents, and perseverance. They are eager to pursue the straight path of truth. The masters are winners because they do not cheat. Therefore, their success is lasting. Lies can seduce people only for a time. Unrighteousness is like an unfaithful friend. It will betray you and abandon you when you most need help. The path of integrity and righteousness is long. But its glory comes from its truth that ultimately prevails.

Many people act as if their life mission is to defeat others. All their energy is wasted in defeating their competitors. Rather than wasting your time in defeating your opponents, work on your attitude in order to bring out the best in yourself. Focus on mastering your skill in order to add quality to your service and products so that you become the master in your expertise.

The winner wants to conquer the world. The winning attitude is to conquer oneself first. Keep in mind that the day you conquer yourself, you are the winner. Dare to burn with a desire to go higher and higher. Not higher than others, but higher than yourself. The masters have conquered themselves first before conquering others. The masters win because they also have a great level of energy and creativity.

Boost Your Energy and Creativity through Relaxation
Many people postpone taking the time to rest. In fact, almost nobody allows himself or others to relax at all. Whether you are a CEO or an employee, if you are just sitting in your chair not doing anything, it looks weird to your team. You have to save face by looking busy all the time. You find it difficult to relax even though you can. In your busy world, if you drop everything, you will feel anxious. You are restless both while doing your activity and while not doing anything.

This reminds me of another story:

It is early morning. The sun is rising. Diogenes, the Greek philosopher, is lying on the sand, on the bank of the river. He is taking a sunbath. Alexander the Great has come to meet Diogenes. During their conversation, Diogenes asks Alexander, "Why do you want to conquer the world? What will you do when you have conquered it?"

Alexander replies, "Perhaps, I will take a rest when I have conquered the world."

The Attitude of the Masters *by Céline Théron*

Diogenes says, "If you want to rest and relax, you can do it here and now." Diogenes had the attitude of a master. He took time to relax. Alexander died never having taken the time to rest.

You deserve to enjoy a restful life. Conquering the whole world is not a necessary step before relaxing. You can relax any time you wish to. Nobody is blocking your path. If you wait until you have achieved all your goals to relax, it will never happen.

Relaxation is necessary, especially in our stressful life. Whenever you find tension increasing, relax. Tension is the beginning of many troubles. Stop rushing. Act as if you have many lives. This gives you a very relaxed attitude towards life.

Relaxation does not necessarily mean doing nothing. It means not being a *doer* and embracing *being* instead. People keep doing and forget *being*. Being is primary and doing is secondary, however. The flowers bloom and the wind keeps blowing. They keep doing. Even though they do a lot, in nature, being is more important than doing.

Energy flows from a peaceful mind and a relaxed body. You become creative in your work when you do not take life so seriously. You do not have to be serious for twenty-four hours a day. Our society teaches us to be that way because it frowns on laugher and frivolity. If you are serious, people think you are valuable. If you laugh a lot, you are not taken seriously. Forget what others think! Allow yourself to relax and laugh.

The source of creativity is an attitude of playfulness which is possible only when you are relaxed. "Eureka! Eureka! I have found it!" the Greek inventor Archimedes cried as he ran naked down the streets of Syracuse. While taking his bath, he made a discovery that was so astounding that he forgot to dress.

The masters unfolded great secrets when their mind was not busy. Great inventions and discoveries happen in a moment of relaxation or playing with soap bubbles. Einstein, Archimedes, Newton, and others either discovered something or found the solution to a problem when they were in a state of playfulness or sleep.

Many things happen when you are in a relaxed state. You have to resist a social standard that forbids rest, laugher, and play. The master is playful and childlike. The master often goes against the current.

Serve before You Seek to Lead

Leading others is not an easy mission. When the boss is kind, the workers see it as a weakness and they won't follow his orders. When the boss is hard, laborers respect him because they fear him. However, if they look up to him instead of fear him they will work harder to please him. You can make people bend by using a sword only for a short period.

The leader has the attitude of the masters. The masters do not use harsh authority as a weapon to control others. As a leader, you can never make someone work efficiently for very long through intimidation. Being a leader does not consist solely of commanding others. Any leader worth being called one knows that he first has to serve before he seeks to lead. He knows how to rule the hearts of others. The mother who disciplines her child with kind words and serves him with affection has more influence than the authoritative father. With your whip, you can make the lions and the tigers to obey you, but you cannot command a bud to blossom.

The master has the attitude of a servant leader. Serving as a leader requires more skill and efficiency than just acting with authority. From an office boy to the CEO, whatever your title is, you are in the service of the company. The leader serves his company by involving employees from different backgrounds.

An emperor used an original method to select his minister. The emperor judged that cooking was a great ability. He thought that a man who knew how to mix different vegetables to make a good meal has the ability to govern the country. So he appointed the cook as his prime minister. Likewise, a good leader in the workplace is someone who knows how to handle all kinds of characters and attitudes of the employees to build a strong team. One cannot make a noise by clapping one hand. It takes both hands. The leader knows that he needs the cooperation of all the employees to achieve any goals.

A true leader is at the service of justice. He allows the laborers to grow according to their potential. He gives credit to them for their efforts and rewards their work. Otherwise, what was not possible to get by hard and honest work will be gotten by mischievous action. As the proverb says, "If man is not allowed to be a lion, he becomes a fox."

In my village, peasants work hard in the rice fields. They are mainly poor women, planting rice saplings in a paddy field. Women's working conditions are difficult. The mothers also have to deal with the constant distraction of their children. The mother has to stop her work and care for them if they are crying. She's afraid that the boss will scold her. After all the pains given to their labor, when the time of reaping the crop comes, they are given a few rupees that barely ease their hunger. They often lament this, saying "They squeeze our blood as juice but we cannot even give one meal per day to our children." One sowed but another reaped. A true leader shares the harvest with everybody so that no one does hard work only to come away feeling unjustly treated.

As a boss, you have to assign a fair price to the work your employees perform. Do not let anyone convince you otherwise. Your good attitude towards the people who work for you is crucial to both the success of the company and to your own success. Your workers are like geese laying golden eggs. If their efforts are not rewarded, they will become unproductive. A leader serves others as he wants to be served. He is responsible for both his team's attitude and for himself.

Responsibility is Freedom
Acting with responsibility is the attitude of a master. Responsibility is freedom. If you take charge of your life as a master, then you can taste freedom. If I'm not responsible for

The Buddha Attitude

myself, then I am not free. But if I am free, then I have to bear the whole responsibility. Freedom and responsibility are two sides of the same coin. Do not throw your responsibility on anyone else or you will be also throwing away your freedom.

You have to assume the responsibility for your work, your company, or your community. Many people never learned to take responsibility. When we were children, our parents took responsibility for us. When you grew up, the situation changed. Now, you have to take your own responsibility. When you refuse to have a responsible attitude, it has an impact on both you and on others.

One day when I was at my primary school in France, I heard the buzzing sound of an insect inside my ear. It was unbearable. During recess, I went to see the teachers who were out walking on the school playground. I told them, "Sir, there is an insect inside my ear."

They all laughed. "You have an insect in your ear?" They asked me, and then they laughed again. They did not want to pay me any attention.

I kept hearing the sound as the fly roamed about inside my ear. It made me feel dizzy. I thought about my sister, Aline, who was in the same school.

She was on the other side of the playground. I went to see her, crying. She took me into the rest room, where she filled her palm with tap water and poured it in my ear. She asked me to bend my head to the side. When I did, the insect fell out, dead. My sister was a child but she solved my problem.

In India, we call school teachers *Master*. That day, my school teachers failed to behave as masters. They failed in their responsibility. They did not keep the children in their care safe.

In some professions, you are responsible for others. Your action or non-action has a consequence. Have a responsible attitude whether you are an executive manager, a doctor, or a student. You have the attitude of the master when you take responsibility for your actions or the omission of actions.

The Attitude of the Masters *by Céline Théron*

Perform Your Work with Joy

The masters perform their work with joy. Make your workplace a festive place. Do your labors joyfully like the farmer singing while he sows seed. Do your work as cheerfully as the gardener who whistles while he plants a shrub. Perform your tasks as happily as the cowherd boy leading the flocks to pasture while playing a flute like Krishna did. These people work to earn their daily food that fills their hunger. In addition, they transform their world into a happy atmosphere that fulfills their spirit.

Today, workers have lost that sense of joy. Change your attitude by turning work into a celebration. Perform your work with a joyful attitude like a master.

Raja Rajan Cholan, one of the most powerful Indian emperors and a devotee of *Shiva*, built the greatest Thanjavur temple nearly a thousand years ago. The entrance to the temple was a high gateway. I once stood before the temple, amazed at this miracle. A divine force that turned the water into wine also worked through the hands of the man who decorated the *gopuram* (tower) with beautiful sculptures. *Nandi*, Shiva's bull, guards the temple. I had never seen such a huge *Nandi* and a large *Shiva Lingam*! A gentle elephant was swinging its trunk near the gate.

The sun was burning. I felt the need for a fresh drink. An old woman wearing a used but clean *saree* was sitting in the doorway of the temple. Her face was shining in the light of the sun. Her grey hair was sticking to her forehead and the sweat was running down her cheeks as she wiped her face with her *saree*. She was selling *mooru* (a salted yogurt drink) in an earthen pot. She welcomed me with a smile. She offered me a tumbler of *mooru* to drink. Her wrinkled eyes expressed a touching affection toward me, a stranger. Her presence refreshed my soul. We conversed quietly. She said, "I am an old woman, seventy-eight years old."

I asked her, "Why do you work in your old age?"

She replied, "With this work, I can have a few rupees.

The Buddha Attitude

With that money, I have the pleasure of buying something for my grandchildren." She was meditative at the gate of the temple and doing her work with reverence. With a wide smile, the little old woman served people passing by the temple with her bony hands. This old woman had the attitude of a master. Despite her old age, she was doing her labor with joy.

Do your work with joy, or out of love. You know how important a job is when you do not have one, so take good care of it when you have the opportunity to work. Some people do not enjoy their work at all. Others tolerate it only because of the income it gives. They would like to get away from their workplace and fly away somewhere. With this attitude, you spoil your life and impede the prosperity of your company. The real satisfaction in life is to work not from compulsion but out of joy. That is what distinguishes man from an ox who also works day and night, all his life, in all circumstances, and under all conditions.

Whatever activity you are doing, perform it with joy. It does not matter whether you are an artist, a scientist, or a sandal maker. There is no such thing as low work. There are only people who have a narrow idea of the value of the labor they perform.

You Do not Have to Be a CEO to do Great Things

Physical activity is good for your well-being. In modern society, machines have replaced humans in many things. Work is now more mental than physical.

Consider this: After a day's toil in the fields, the peasant returns home. He washes his feet and hands. He picks up the water jug and drinks fresh water. After his light evening meal, his wife prepares a mat, his bed. He immediately falls asleep tired in body, but with peace of mind. He sleeps deeply until morning. When was the last time you had a good rest like this? Working in an office is not enough. You need physical work to be relaxed. You can go for a walk, go for a run, or go swimming. Anything that gets your body moving is good for your mind and your physical health.

The Attitude of the Masters *by Céline Théron*

Manual labor has its value. Unfortunately, many people consider it a disgrace to perform it.

Do not think that you have to be a CEO to do great things. A great man brings great quality to everything he does. All men's work contributes to prosperity on earth. It is your servant that gives you the honorable title of master. Our daily food is the harvest of a peasant in the fields. The costly wood furniture comes from the hard work of a woodcutter. The beautiful embroidered mango design textile comes from the weaving of soft hands. The smooth road on which an expensive car is driven is paved by brave workmen. The clean streets of our neighborhood are the worthy work of the road sweeper. The value of manual labor is not in the nature of the work but in the attitude of the worker.

Manual labor is not a curse. The sweat of your hard work will wash away the misfortune written on your forehead. Village girls carry water in their earthen pots from the wellspring. Young boys fetch wood from the hills. But they are unhappy doing such ordinary things. They curse their perceived destiny that they are condemned to doing small things. They think they are unlucky living a poor little existence. It is not the work that makes them miserable but the feeling that they are doing unimportant work. But you are not your work, so do not evaluate yourself according to the nature of it.

The masters have a respectful attitude toward their work. Whether you are a farmer, a fisherman, a carpenter, or a shoemaker, it does not matter. The work of a street cleaner is as important as that of the king on his throne. One who is ashamed of his work does not respect himself.

That does not mean that you should not aim for a better position in life. Your current place is your jumping board. If you go on cursing it, you cannot take a leap. If you are unhappy where you are standing now, then the soil will tear you down as if it were quicksand. Instead, stand firmly on the ground to make the next step and move ahead.

The Buddha Attitude

A promising future can be born only from your present. If you are a woodcutter, do not be ashamed of your labor. Do not compare it to the position of the president of a country. A beautiful future will be born out of your positive attitude to the present moment. Who you are today is not who you are going to be tomorrow. In the annals of history, you can find proof that a man who worked as a woodcutter and taught himself to read went on to become an exceptional leader. He was one of the Presidents of the United States. His name: Abraham Lincoln. He was never ashamed to say in public that his father, Thomas Lincoln, was a farmer and a carpenter.

Put Your Heart into Your Work!

Do not work only with your mind. Put your heart into your work. Then, your work can be a joy. When you are simply doing your work for the sake of doing and your heart is not in it, you are wasting your energy. One should not work only to earn a living. Work should provide a living and the joy of living. Enjoy doing what you do.

If you detest your labor, walk away. Hence, you won't waste your time and your company's investment in you. Lead your life as a master by doing what you like to do. Many people did not choose their career. Someone else did it for them. Their parents wanted them to be a doctor, a lawyer, or an engineer. So, they went through school to become what their parents expected. Or they do work that is praised by society. As they are doing something that they never wanted to do, they feel unfulfilled in their work. You cannot stay for a long time in a position where you do not fit in. With courage, you can always find something that you like to do for a future job.

Quitting work is not easy for many of us. Why is it so hard to quit? Leaving a job means you have to face new difficulties. You have doubts that maybe you won't like the new situation or your new job will not pay so much. You cannot get something from nothing. A little less salary and a little more inconvenience will be better if you are happy doing your new job. What is the use of earning so much money if your work is not meaningful for you?

Focus on Your Work Instead of the Results
Our natural attitude is to expect results from our work. Any activity or work has to bring something in return. Working without expecting results means having patience and being mature enough to wait for results. The *Gita* (Hindu scripture) says, "Do your duty without worrying about the results. For the result is interwoven with the very act."

The masters know to focus on their work instead of the results. Focus is the key to success. We are living in a world of distractions. Television, internet, radio, and traffic are constantly screaming at us. The reality is most people are too easily distracted. They are looking for the next best thing. When it comes to mastery or becoming the best in your field, your attitude should be like digging for gold. At first, you will shovel a lot of dirt. But with focus and patience, you will eventually strike gold. Do not keep jumping to the next plot of land to dig for it if you fail to find gold after turning a few shovelfuls of earth. It takes laser-like focus and incredible patience to achieve your goal and get the desired results.

Concentrate on your work. When one works with concentration, losing all consciousness of ourselves, the work that is done will be infinitely better.

A potter is shaping his craft. He concentrates his whole attention on his craft. He loses consciousness of everything else for the time being. His mind, hands, and eyes are all focused on his work. He turns the wheel and the clay whirls round. Out of clay, he creates an earthen pot, a pottery jug, plates, or a lamp. The master's hands have turned the clay into art. What was mud a few moments ago is now a beautiful object that people will pay to own. The flowers do not seek for bees; they come by themselves to suck the honey. So are good quality items that attract customers in a shop.

If the craftsman thinks about what price he is going to

The Buddha Attitude

sell his craft while at his wheel, the shape of his pottery will be deformed in the end. But if he simply concentrates on his work, he gets a good price when he puts it up for sale. So do not think about the promotion you will get if you finish a project, the raise of your salary for the task you are doing, or the price for which you will sell your products. Concentrate on your work instead of the results and you *will* be rewarded for your good work.

Some people are tired of working hard and not getting any results. A great Indian sage named Thiruvalluvar says, "Something may not be achievable even by God or through God's help. But the effort exerted to attain that non-achievable will yield its deserving result!" In the world, no conscious work is ever wasted. Sooner or later, someone must pay you for it. When you do your work with a high level of quality, the results are bound to happen. Even the least thing done well brings marvelous results.

Your work has a high quality to it when you do it with an attitude of *seva*. *Seva* is a service which is performed without any expectation of result or reward by the person performing it. Adopting an attitude of *seva* might seem unrewarding. But give it a second thought to understand its deep meaning.

Once a king passed by an old man planting an olive tree. The king was surprised by the old man's actions. "Why are you planting this tree? You will never benefit from its fruits." The king asked the old man.

The old man replied, "Past generations planted trees. I enjoyed the fruits of them all my life. Now, I plant a tree for the benefit of those who will come after me."

The king, astonished by the answer, rewarded the old man with gold coins. The old man thanked the king and said, "It is the first time I have seen a plant bear fruit as soon as I planted it!"

That is the attitude of a master. He does the work for work's sake.

The secret of true success, and of true happiness, then,

is this: Do the work for its own sake without expecting any return, even if such a belief seems like a paradox to you. Give what you have to give, and it will come back to you multiplied as the echo returns your voice several times.

Never Rush the Process; Growth is Slow

In our modern society, people are so impatient that everything must happen fast for them. Patience has become an old-fashioned virtue. Like in *The Sorcerer's Apprentice,* people want the magic to happen before they are fully trained. But whoever aspires to be a master should first be a disciple.

Growth is a slow process. For example, a coconut tree takes years to grow. Be patient with it. In due time, this tree bears fruit that will quench your thirst with fresh, sweet water. It will also give you milk for cooking and leaves for the roof of your shelter. Finally, its large palms can offer you protection from the sun with their shade.

All that is beautiful and great takes time. For example, if you want to learn to play music it will take years of practice to master it. Experience comes from practice. To achieve mastery, you have to practice a lot. Mastery is an attitude. All masters have one common denominator: They spent hours painfully mastering their craft.

Are you ready to be the best? Then have an obsession to master your craft. The best people in sports, arts, and business all share an obsession to master their craft. Their attitude about it is very different from the average person. Read the biographies of the masters and you will discover that they always had a passion for their craft even at an early age. They did not choose to go into their profession because the money was good. They earned the admiration of others because their talent had become natural and spontaneous. They cannot explain their talent by techniques. It is as mystical as the centipede's skill in using a hundred legs at once.

If you want to become a master, you need incredible patience before creating a masterpiece. One of the greatest

The Buddha Attitude

masters in music, Mozart, said, "It is a mistake to think that the practice of my art has become easy to me. I assure you, dear friend, no one has given so much care to the study of composition as I. There is scarcely a famous master in music whose works I have not frequently and diligently studied."

Work with Reverence

Great artists found in their creation God's revelation. Beethoven said, "No friend have I. I must live by myself alone; but I know well that God is nearer to me than others in my art, so I will walk fearlessly with Him." In his work, Beethoven saw God. But you do not need to be a great artist to do your work with reverence.

Work is worship. The masters worship their work.

The mystic poet and saint of India, Kabir, was a weaver by profession. They say that when Kabir went to sell his cloth in Kashi, he would go dancing. He said, "The cloth that I make is made not just to sell but to serve God, to serve existence in the way in which I can serve it the best."

He met the divine in each and every customer. He called his customer "Rama," the name of his God. When Kabir sold something to a customer, he would say, "Rama, I have been weaving for you. I have worked very hard spinning this. Take good care of it. I have woven it in such a way that it should give you good service throughout your whole life. It should serve your children as well."

Have the attitude of the masters. Have an attitude of reverence toward your work. Treat your workplace as sacred. The tree is known by its fruits. The mother is known by her child. The quality of your work is known by your attitude toward your work. Whatever task you perform, do it with reverence. When you put your very soul into your work–whether you are cleaning, weaving or plowing–you create something of a divine quality like Beethoven.

Here is another story which has a valuable lesson:

The sun is burning. Laborers are working hard on a

The Attitude of the Masters *by Céline Théron*

temple which is under construction near a city gate.

An old man passing by looks at one of the laborers who carries a load of bricks on his head and asks, "What are you doing?"

"Don't you see? I am carrying bricks." The laborer replied in an irritated tone without looking at the old man.

The old man repeated the question to another laborer. "I am earning a living for my family." This laborer replied in a low, sad voice.

The old man finally approached a third laborer, a young man who carried bricks on his head with a happy look on his face. "What are you doing, my child?" The old man asked him. "I am building a temple." The happy laborer gracefully replied.

The three labors are doing the same work but their attitude towards their work is different. The first two disliked their work, but the third workman has turned the task of carrying bricks into a sacred task. He had the attitude of the masters.

When you work with a reverent attitude, your heart is fulfilled. Bring to your work a divine quality. Sell the earthen pots as if they are an offering to a deity. Weave clothes as if you are a mother preparing garments for her child. Complete your day-to-day work with diligence as if you are preparing a dinner for your beloved.

Detach Yourself from Your Work

A detached attitude is important to doing a good job. Detachment does not mean indifference. With a detached attitude, you will not work out of fear.

Consider this situation: A lawyer is afraid of the ending of the case in which his dearest friend is involved. The question arises in his mind: *Will I win or not?* With other clients, he gave his defense speech without being emotionally affected. Now, his emotions disturb his mind. In the same way, a great doctor will not be able to operate efficiently on a member of his family. His emotional involvement does not help him to do the

The Buddha Attitude

operation without fear of failing. He was natural with other patients. Now he hesitates.

Work as a master with a detached attitude. Your work is not your identity. When people are fired, they become desperate. They go so far as to put an end to their life. That is because they identified themselves with their work. And by losing their work, they also lost their identity. So when it comes to you and your work, be instead like a soldier who, once called upon for war, leaves his home, friends, village or city to go on an adventure from which he does not even know if he will return home. Work with a detached attitude for the good of your company and for yourself.

CHAPTER TWO

Do Not Fight With Darkness

Do Not Fight With Darkness

———⋅◦⋐⋑◦⋅———

In town, noisy streets are full of the sounds of cars. Auto rickshaw horns blare and bicycle bells tinkle. These sounds meld together with beautiful background music. Along the sidewalks, various shops are lined with people. Among the crowd, in the bumps and holes, the gentle cow is lying quietly. Huge flower garlands of yellow, crimson, and green decorate the flower shops. The busy Indian market is teeming with life, full of bright colors, and the tantalizing smells of fresh fruits, vegetables, spices, incense, tumeric roots, and kumkum.

It is market day. The folks from all the villages around have come to buy and sell. Women sell flowers in the market, outside the temple, or on the street corners. Every time I go there, I buy beautiful fresh flowers from those kind ladies. They have many baskets of different flowers including jasmines, crossandras, and carnations. We can smell the fragrance of these flowers from a distance. However, if there is foul water running by the sidewalk, it gives off a stench that smothers the perfume of these many flower baskets.

Similarly, a person with a negative attitude can spread negative energy around you no matter how positive you are. He or she tears you down. He or she ruins your good reputation. As fast as you build, he or she destroys. When you are constantly around people who have negative attitudes, you are living in darkness. Darkness is only the absence of light. To come out of this darkness, you simply need to light the candle of wisdom to become aware of negative influences on you. The moment you are conscious that some people have a bad impact on you, disconnect from them and walk away.

It takes courage to say, "This relationship is unhealthy!" and to make the decision to untie the knot that ties you to that poisonous relationship. A bad relationship is like a silk shawl that gets caught in the thorns of a rosebush. You try to pick the thorns from the shawl or to you try to get the shawl away from the thorns; either way, a piece of the silk can be torn. In the same way, when you get rid of a bad relationship or try to distance yourself from it, it affects you. Hence, you have to be cautious and careful.

Avoid Touching the Gypsy Moth

One day back when I was a child, I went to play in our garden after a rainstorm. Once I was in the garden, I held out my hand to catch the raindrops falling like crystals from the banana leaves of a tree that stood next to it. Suddenly, I felt something on my foot. I looked down, and saw a gypsy moth. Being very young, I was afraid of that insect. Many times I had stepped on it with my bare foot or mistakenly touched it. Gypsy moths always gave me an itchy rash that could last several days. Like the gypsy moth, negative-minded people can have an irritating effect on you. Coming into contact with them is like the itch of a gypsy moth. Worse, the irritation they give you leaves a lasting effect because their negativity saps your energy.

When was the last time you walked away silently from a person who tried to irritate you or to get you into an

Do Not Fight With Darkness

argument? Do not fight with them. Instead, simply walk away, because trying to reason with them is as foolish as arguing with a drunkard. You need the attitude of the masters to walk away. Because walking away instead of fighting requires great spiritual strength.

Keep Your Distance from Bad Company

My sister attended the village's elementary school just a few steps from our home in India. Whenever I passed by the school, I often heard children singing. I still remember a line from one of the songs they sang: "Keep distance from people doing evil." Through that song the teacher taught the children to get into a friendship with positive people.

Unfortunately, many people cling to an unhealthy friendship even though they know it is not good for them. Do not be tempted to try to change those friends. No one can change anyone else, and it is a waste of time to try to reform people who have a negative attitude. The masters know that they should keep away from bad company. Gandhi, who once tried to reform a friend, said, "A reformer cannot afford to have close intimacy with him whom he seeks to reform (...) for man takes in vice far more readily than virtue."

Choose your friends carefully. False friends have a selfish attitude. They are like swallows that visit during nice weather but fly away as soon as winter is on the way. They are only your friends during the good times. Walk away from those who do not deserve to be called friends.

Bad company is not only phony friends. People you trust as your good advisors or your "drivers" can also be bad company. Your driver is the person to whom you have given the right to direct your life, and to guide you. It is not easy to discover that these people whom you trusted have misdirected you from the right path. You don't need to be harsh with people who are bad company, but you must always keep your distance from them.

The Attitude of the Masters *by Céline Théron*

Do Not Try to Drive Them Away

I have always dreamed of seeing the Taj Mahal. During my vacation, I traveled to Agra to visit this marvelous monument, one of the Seven Wonders of the World. As it was a tourist place, many teenagers hawked souvenirs at the place where tourists boarded carriages to take them to the Taj Mahal. One such boy followed the people who came along with me until we got into the carriage that waited for us. He insisted that we buy from him. The lady who sat next to me insulted him. The boy's eyes blazed with anger. But he controlled himself. He told me, "This lady is mean. I do not understand her language, but I am clever. I know she said harsh words to me."

I was silent. I did not know how to control that lady and console the boy. I gave him money. He refused it, saying, "I'm selling souvenirs. I am not a beggar." He calmly walked away at that point. The boy had the attitude of a master. He decided to walk away with serenity from people having a negative attitude.

My longtime dream ended there. The lady who had been rude to the boy destroyed my dream as a result because after that incident, I did not have the heart to visit the Taj Mahal. I was right in the shadow of this fascinating monument but I could not enjoy it, for my thoughts lingered on the boy who was hurt. Even in his poverty, he had a great sense of dignity. Whatever the situation is, a lofty man will never lose the richness of his soul. As an Indian proverb says, "Even in hunger, a tiger will not eat grass." The boy's attitude was proof of the wisdom of this saying.

This incident also changed my attitude. I vowed never to sit next to a dream destroyer again.

You need to walk away as calmly as this boy if you are with a person who prevents you from living your dream or impedes the progress of your life. Trying to drive that person away would be difficult. What we try to get rid of has the tendency to stick to us, much like how an angry dog pursues you even when you throw stones at it. So always walk away instead.

But sometimes, it is hard to walk away from some people. They might be someone to whom you are attached or that you depend upon.

Be Like a Crab in the Mud

I remember when I was a child I played in the rice fields in my neighborhood. Crabs live along the sides of the terraces in the fields. I used to watch them coming and going in all directions before digging into mud holes. I usually spent some time trying to catch them. Just as I almost seized a crab, they hid themselves from my sight. I caught one, put it back in water, and made a new attempt. These games went on like this until my mother sent somebody to remind me that it was time for my meal.

You can learn from the crabs' lifestyle. Crabs have something peculiar about them. Even though they live in mud, you can't see any trace of it on their shell. In the same way, even when you are being with people who have a bad attitude, you can remain positive. Do not give to people with negative attitudes the power to leave a trace on your mind, so create a mental distance from them. You protect your inner peace that way. You cannot change a person with a bad attitude, but, you can change your attitude towards them.

Throw away Your Spear

A king had been at war with a man for many years. The king fought many battles against him without a victory. In their last battle, the king defeated his old enemy. The man fell to the ground. His face was covered with dust. The king sat on his enemy's chest, raised his spear, and prepared to kill him.

Then the king's old enemy spat in the king's face.

The king threw away his spear and stood up.

His old enemy was puzzled. He asked, "After many years, you have defeated me. Why have you decided not to kill me?"

The king replied, "You are not my equal. By spitting in my face, you have shown such pettiness that it would be

The Attitude of the Masters *by Céline Théron*

disgraceful for me to kill such a weak person who could only spit at me." Then, the king gracefully walked away from the battlefield with his head held high.

The attitude of the master is like that of the king. The attitude of the master is noble. Refusing to fight, although in a position to do so, is great power. When the adversary does not have any class, do not get involved with him in any way. The exchange should be with people of equal values.

Fighting exists everywhere: between parents and children, husband and wife, boss and servant, lover and beloved, stranger and stranger, nation and nation. Nothing is extraordinary in fighting, but there is strength in throwing away the spear. The attitude of the master is not adopting cheap manners. Walk away with dignity from pettiness.

People with negative attitudes are living in darkness. If you go on fighting with them or criticizing them, you will also remain in darkness. Do not fight with darkness. Rather, light a candle to dissipate the darkness. People with negative attitudes are good teachers. We can learn from their attitudes. Abbe Pierre, the French humanitarian, said, "Everyone does what they want of their life. Some drag it in the mud. How are they soiling ours? They are showing us how one can render it despicable. Let's learn from them and let's make it splendid!"

CHAPTER THREE

Your Intimate Enemy Is Fear

Your Intimate Enemy Is Fear

My sister Aline and I had to walk a long distance to buy raw milk when we lived in our village. Many people drank a pitcher of hot milk in the evening. The neighbours had one cow or a goat. They could not provide milk for the entire village.

The sun was like a furnace. We had not seen a drop of rain for many months. We walked through the narrow unpaved roads of the village. Women passed by carrying bundles of wood on their heads. At a corner, we stood in the shade of a tamarind tree to let the shepherd pass by as he was bringing the sheep back from gazing. The flock and its guide disappeared. The street was empty. We continued on our way to get milk.

At one point on our walk we had to pass through a Kali temple. Kali is the four-armed fierce goddess with blue skin. She has very long and messy black hair. Her tongue is sticking out. She wears a garland of skulls around her neck. We were told that human sacrifices were offered to Kali. As kids, we were frightened whenever we approached the temple. The

The Attitude of the Masters *by Céline Théron*

fear increased as we got nearer to the temple. My sister Aline always held my hand to help me run fast. We ran until we reached a distance far from the temple. Today, I know that the story about human sacrifices was a rumor. But the fear that rumor gave me penetrated deep into my young heart.

Revisit Your Old Beliefs

Fear is something we pick up through life because of either an incident that happened to us, or due to social constraints, or because of old customs.

The elderly people in my village had accumulated old beliefs that they still followed, such as: if you were leaving home and saw a widow or a barren woman, you would get back luck.

God has created millions of flowers on this earth. But He hasn't created a flower as beautiful and soft as a woman. In fact, India is depicted as a woman. Then, how can seeing a woman even though she is a widow or barren be unlucky? Celebrate a woman as a goddess. The personification of India is *Bhārata Mātā* (Mother India.) In my country, the mother is representative of god. Then can a son or a daughter consider their or someone else's widowed mother bad luck? A barren woman might not have given birth physically, but she might be born with maternal instincts. Motherhood should be glorified in all its shapes.

Elderly people sowed all kind of fears. Their superstitious attitude created fear in people's minds, especially us kids. We were told not to go outside at specific times of the afternoon, because this was the time when the bad spirits wandered. The air was always heavy at that time. Adults took a nap during those hours. The streets were deserted. The shops were closed. It was a time of fearful silence for all of us. If we went to play outside, people frightened us by saying that a ghost was balancing on a neem tree. They frightened us to the point we became timid.

The days had grown shorter. Night fell earlier. I was told that midnight was the most dangerous time. I was also told that when a dog barked, it meant that a thief or a cat was approaching the house or that when a dog howled, spirits were roving nearby, or that a dog's howling at night also foretold death.

The night was filled with the noise of spirits to me. The groaning of the dead and the cry of the owl disturbed my sleep. Dread touched me deeply with its frightening fingers. Then, a branch cracked or the shadow of a lizard darted across the wall and turned nighttime into a private nightmare for me.

Many of the beliefs people held were spawned by things that happened in their past, while other beliefs are still followed only out of habit. Nevertheless, we still hold close some fears that are not supposed to exist. We cling to them as if they are our heritage.

The Village Guardian Deity

People in the village liked to gossip into the wee hours of the night. Elderly people who were present talked about life in former times. They would tell us stories either about Hindu mythology, ancient kings, great men, or about God and mysterious phenomena. Adults and children, leaning with our cheeks resting on their hands, listened intently to their amazing stories.

My father also told people stories from his experiences in foreign lands. I was impressed by his various stories, all of which left their mark on my memory. He also told us about strange experiences that had happened to him, and about the deity named Ayyannar. Ayyannar was the guardian who protected all of the rural villages. The Ayyannar temple is often far from the village in a desert place. This deity has a fearful face. He is seen riding a horse and brandishing a sword. It is said that, at night, he goes on his rounds around the village to protect it.

We often laughed at that belief. My father was not superstitious, but he told us not to laugh at that story.

The Attitude of the Masters *by Céline Théron*

My dad had a rice field. To protect it during the harvest season, he went to sleep in a shelter built on it. One night, he awakened to a strange noise. It sounded as if there was a crowd riding horses. In the distance, he could see a shape on horseback holding a fiery torch. He quickly hid because the horsemen were coming in his direction. It is said that if someone is in front of Ayyannar when he goes on his rounds with his escorts, that person will die. My dad returned home quickly that night.

Fear is a Ghost

Some people left their homes in the morning and reached home by walking at midnight. They walked on the path, trusting in the light of the moon and the stars to show the way. These people claimed to have seen strange creatures on the streets at that time. Some even had such an adverse reaction to what they thought they saw that they died of a heart attack. Many people also told of seeing dead people coming back to visit their families. My dad confirmed to me that he had had the same experience.

For example, in my neighborhood a kind young man once died by accident. My dad was sorry that he had died so young. One night, my father returned home looking sad. Mama asked him what the matter was. My dad said that he had seen the young man sitting outside his hut. He asked the young man, "Why are you sitting there, my boy?" It is believed that when a person died young, by accident, before their appointed time, they wandered for a while.

Do not carry dead corpses with you because you are a living man. If you believe in the dead, you believe in death, not life. If you want to be alive, do not live in fear. Be with the living and you will become more alive.

Fear is a ghost that we have to chase away in order to purify the air. Give up the ghost so you can live fully without fear. We often grow up with fears. Those childhood fears give way to adult fears of change, business failure, or rejection. Look at

Your Intimate Enemy Is Fear

the fear that follows you as a ghost that you have to wipe away from your mind.

Uproot Your Fear

Strangely enough, it seems that we always want to hear ghost stories again and again even as adults. Otherwise, how can we explain the success of horror movies?

In my village, people who had to come back home after a late-night walk always avoided seeing scary movies. Even those people were fascinated when the movie *The Exorcist* was released in the town theatre. We like the feelings created by horror movies. We are attracted by supernatural experiences. Somehow, we are bored with normal life. Everything that triggers our imagination becomes interesting.

Fear is not something to cultivate. Uproot it! Yank it out the way you'd uproot weeds. You always have to pull out weeds and throw them away. Otherwise, the weeds will hinder the growth of vegetables and flowers in your garden. In the same way, if you do not uproot fear from your mind, it will impede your spiritual growth.

Fear blocks us from realizing our full potential. If you try to do something in fear, you can get a negative result. You will not explore new lands, ideas, directions, or aspirations because of fear. You will always live the same safe lifestyle, follow the same pattern, or walk the same path again and again. The masters do not let fears prevent them from taking a new route.

Fear Can Distort Your Reality

When you are living in fear, imagination plays an important role. My dad told us about his life in the army during the war. He described how he once had to hide in the tomato fields. He remained lying on the ground for many days because of enemy attacks. Having nothing to eat, he ate tomatoes for fifteen days.

He told us this story of a soldier during war time: Once, a

The Attitude of the Masters *by Céline Théron*

superior officer was killed in the war. The army kept his body until they could return it to his family.

A soldier had to guard the dead body of the officer at night. All night he was alone with the dead body. Suddenly, the guard heard a strange noise coming from close to the dead person. He looked around. There was nobody there. He could not understand this mysterious noise which occurred intermittently with short periods of silence in between. The soldier was so terrified that he was not able to sleep that night. All kinds of fearful thoughts assailed him.

In the morning, the soldiers discovered that the noise had come from the seedpods that had dropped from a tree that towered over the shelter where the dead body lay. The shelter had a metal roof. As seedpods dropped on the metal roof of the shelter, the soldier heard the noises he thought were coming from close to the officer's corpse.

The soldier who was not afraid to be killed in a war lost his sleep because of the noise of objects falling on a roof. His imagination ran away with him, creating a scary situation. When you face problems in life, do not let your imagination get carried away. It will show you a situation that is worse than in reality. Your imagination will raise your anxiety about many things that will never even happen in reality.

We often worry unnecessarily. We live in an imaginary world of unfounded fears. We go on spinning and weaving new worries, new fears. We are tremendously efficient at creating anxiety and anguish. In fear, you do not have an objective attitude. You let your imagination run wild. The soldier had nothing to be worried about but his imagination created a terrifying scene. There was no real danger near him, but his fear was real. That is the problem with fear: It can kill you from inside if you do not control it.

Fear Can Kill You

I am reminded of something that happened at a circus in India. It concerned a man who was in charge of cleaning a lion's cage. The cage had two large chambers and a gate in between so as to secure the man from the lion's attack while cleaning the cage.

Before opening the circus to the public, the man routinely cleaned the lion's cage. He would first clean the empty side of the chamber while the lion was in the other chamber. Then he got out and opened the divider to let the lion move onto the cleaned side. Then he closed the divider and cleaned the other side.

One day, he made a fatal mistake. He did not close the gate properly. The lion opened the gate with its paws. The man froze. The lion lay in front of him, staring at him without blinking.

A crowd gathered around the cage. They felt powerless to help the man. They informed the owner of the circus about what had happened. He was reluctant to shoot the lion before exploring other ways to rescue the man. They tried to divert the lion's attention. They offered it fresh meat. The lion was not tempted. It did not take its eyes off the man.

When they finally got the lion under control, they checked on the man in the cage. They discovered that he had been dead for quite a long time even though the lion did not attack him. Fear killed him. Fear can kill you if you do not control it.

What fears frighten you like they were a lion? Masters know how to face their fears. They do not let fears terrify them. Have the attitude of the masters. Face your fear with a courageous attitude. Courage does not mean absence of fear. Courage is the attitude of a person who acknowledges the fear, puts it aside, and goes ahead. He is taking a risk. You need tremendous courage to face the unknowns of life.

Change is Permanent

Change is the Law of Nature. Change is permanent. Everything else is temporary. The earth constantly changes each moment as the day turns into night. Change is everywhere. Change is also invisible in many things because it is so

The Attitude of the Masters *by Céline Théron*

subtle and slow. Even though everything is changing all the time, people fear change. There is a strong conservative tendency in the human attitude towards change because we do not like it. Why is change so difficult? It pulls you from the known to the unknown, from the secure to the insecure, from your comfortable world to an uneasy life.

From early childhood, we are afraid of change. A child cannot always stay at home. When the time is right, he should move from home to school. I have seen many children refusing to go to school, clinging to their mothers desperately. I was one of them.

I never forgot my first day of school. When I turned five years old, I had to leave home to go to school for the first time. Mama awakened me early. She had bought me a beautiful white cotton dress so that I could feel cooler in the hot weather we were having at the time. She prepared my favorite breakfast, *dosai* and coconut chutney.

I kissed Mama on both cheeks. I started crying when I left her. The school was in town, a little far from my village in India. My dad put me on the back of his bicycle to ride me to school. When I saw the gateway leading into the school I began to get scared, because I saw a bunch of strangers inside.

I said, "Dad, I don't want to stay here by myself."

I will never forget how reassuring my dad's voice was as he said to me, "Honey, don't stay alone. Go and sit with the other children. Face your fear. You're going to be just fine." And I was.

Change your attitude towards change. Embrace it instead of fear it. The attitude of the masters is the opposite of the common attitude of people. They embrace change all along their lives. Life is all about embracing change. Without change you cannot grow. Once you understand that, you will not be afraid of change. Life is about change.

Everything that is alive is changing. Only dead things never change. Change is insecurity, and we all are searching for security. But insecurity is the very soul of life, the very nature of life. There are no guarantees in life.

Your Intimate Enemy Is Fear

I am reminded of the vagabond. He walked miles through the woods. He heard the howling of hungry wolves. After nightfall, the path was no longer visible. The vagabond was hungry. In the distance, he could see a dim light. When he approached it, he found a hut. So he halted at that lonely house in which a light was burning and knocked on the door. An old woman who carried a light appeared. He told her, "I'm lost and I'm very tired. Please allow me to stay in your hut overnight."

The old lady let him sleep in her hut. When morning dawned, he woke up. A mysterious, frightening surprise was waiting for him: The hut and the old lady had disappeared, and he now found himself in a graveyard.

The moral of this story is that when you are sleeping peacefully in your comfort zone, you are not conscious that you are sleeping in a graveyard. Every time you fear change and choose to remain in a secure place, you are standing in a graveyard. When there is no change, the ground you tread is a grave, a place where there is no life for you. So embrace change no matter what pain it may give you at first.

Change is Painful

In my village, there was an *Ant Hill* (Snake's Home) in a wild park. People worshipped *Naga* (snake). Mama took me with her to the park. She gave a *pooja* (ritual) to the snakes. She offered milk and egg to a cobra. This reverence for all the creatures of God is something Mother taught me from earliest childhood.

While Mama was giving the *pooja*, I was playing nearby, trying to touch a shy plant to see how it would shrink. When I saw a discarded skin, I realized that the cobra was somewhere nearby. The cobra had recently shed a layer of its skin.

A snake will shed its skin to allow for continued growth. When a snake outgrows it, it simply sheds the outer layer. In place of the old skin is a more vibrant and fresh skin. The process of shedding is painful. Just as a snake slips out of the

The Attitude of the Masters *by Céline Théron*

old skin and does not even look back, you have to leave behind layer by layer your old habits and embrace change. Change is very difficult because your old beliefs and fears have to be dropped. A change in your attitude is necessary to get rid of old ways. It is not like clothes that you can easily change. Not fearing change means embracing what life brings to you. Life is unpredictable. We do not know what is going to happen next. Life is full of surprises. That's part of its beauty. Accept change and start a new life.

Explore the Unknown

The unknown is part of the wonder of life. Columbus sailed to an unknown world and he discovered a new land. Life is an adventure. Go through it as an explorer.

I had to explore a new land once: France. I had to leave my dog, my familiar landscape, and, temporarily, my Mama. The change was drastic. In the city of Paris, everything was new and strange: the people, their manners, their style of dress, tall towers and big concrete buildings, and huge supermarkets. The different tempo of life in Paris took away my happiness. I could not help thinking about my mother's love. My separation from her deeply distressed me. I felt so sad I fell sick. I also missed Mother Nature and playing with animals. One day, I was so happy to see a familiar bird in Paris when a crow strutted about in the garden.

I had to change my attitude and adapt to many things. For example, French food was a serious problem. I refused to eat for many days because I was not accustomed to it. I had not seen the French baguette before. Mama used to serve me Indian bread, *roty*, with fresh butter she had prepared. I saw baguette in my school canteen for the first time. I thought that it was something to eat with a knife and fork. So I picked up a piece with my fork and put it on my plate. I cut and ate it. All the children looked at me strangely because of the way I ate my first piece of baguette. The main meal was accompanied by potatoes. I observed children eating potatoes with a sauce.

So I served myself a big spoonful of that sauce. I mixed a potato with it and ate.

Suddenly, tears flowed down on my face. I dropped the fork. I drank a glass of water in one gulp, then a second, then a third. The children at the table got scared and the called the school canteen supervisor who came running and asked, "Céline, what happened? Do you feel bad? Do you want to go to the infirmary?"

I could not speak. I continued crying. Then he looked at my plate. He understood the problem. The sauce I had eaten was called "mustard." I learned to use it with caution from that day forward.

I had to learn everything about the new culture I was in to adapt to it, and so I had my first experience in exploring the unknown. When you cling to the known, you move in a circle repeating your past. The unknown should beckon you because you haven't lived it yet. It is unexplored territory and an exciting, new experience may happen there. An open attitude to exploring the unknown will help you to evolve. Choose the unknown no matter what the risk is and you will grow continuously. The unknown can only challenge you, and it can happen at any time, so always be ready to face it.

Live Dangerously

The masters live dangerously eager to face any critical situations thanks to their inner strength. Live dangerously as a master. Wake up your inner power. When you are in danger, the power which is hidden in you awakens. Your energy and potency arise to face a dangerous situation. During war time, a grocer of a tiny village suddenly becomes a hero. To defend itself or its kittens, a house cat can become as fierce as a tiger.

I have always been amazed by my friend in India, Lakshmi, the temple elephant. I am the first lady that she carried on her back. She is smart and gentle. People came from all over the world to see Lakshmi. This giant creature with its large limbs is capable of picking up the tiniest needle from the ground.

The Attitude of the Masters *by Céline Théron*

She can also uproot a tall tree. Lakshmi had a chain around her foot. I was surprised to see that she has never broken it. From the time she was a baby elephant, she had always worn it. As a result, she is not free in her mind.

You are the same as Lakshmi in that you are unaware of the strength that is within you. If you break the chain of fear, you can attain your full potential.

The secret of getting the best from life is to live dangerously. Many people fear tomorrow. Not to be afraid of tomorrow is living dangerously; it is living as a master. Never fear what will become of you.

Unexpected disaster passed through the gate of our village once. A violent storm opened its mouth like a ferocious, yawning beast. It swallowed up cows, sheep, and fowls. Everything disappeared under the water. The strong wind took away the roofs of the huts. Many villagers soon found themselves as without shelter as birds who have lost their nests. The villagers little cooking fires had been dowsed by the water, so their stomachs were empty. The storm had devastated them in body and spirit. Women lamented. Kids cried and hid behind their mothers' arms. The men stood looking helplessly at the destruction around them. They took refuge outside the village in the ruins of an old temple where there were no gates, just walls, all of which were falling down. A small piece of roof was still intact. And so those people were left as ruined as that temple worn by sun and rain.

It is hard to predict what will occur tomorrow. You do not know what is going to destroy your possessions. Today you have a home; tomorrow you could lose it. Today you have a job; tomorrow you might not have one. Today you have money; tomorrow you may be penniless. Today you have friends; tomorrow you could face loneliness. There is no certainty about tomorrow.

Have a courageous attitude toward life. Go through life like the village guardian, holding in one hand a lamp and in the other a strong stick to keep the villagers safe. Your courage

Your Intimate Enemy Is Fear

will help you to cross the road despite whatever the obstacles that you might encounter. As the guardian of night, when it is dark, raise the lantern. When you sense danger, use your strong stick.

Consider the feeble rose dancing in a strong windstorm without fear. Except man, nothing in Nature is miserable thinking about what will happen tomorrow. When Nature cries, it nourishes the earth. Living things on earth grow. When man cries, Nature laughs. Live for today and do not be afraid of tomorrow. Believe in life. It will take care of you.

CHAPTER FOUR
Your Faithful Servant

Your Faithful Servant

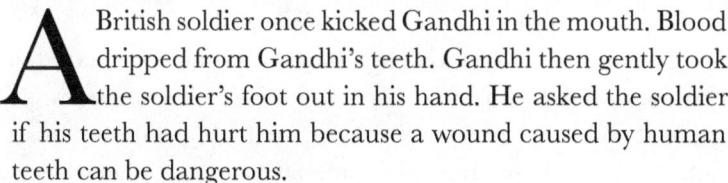

A British soldier once kicked Gandhi in the mouth. Blood dripped from Gandhi's teeth. Gandhi then gently took the soldier's foot out in his hand. He asked the soldier if his teeth had hurt him because a wound caused by human teeth can be dangerous.

In this situation, people would normally feel humiliated. However, Mahatma Gandhi had the attitude of a master. He was not ashamed of what the soldier did but he was worried for him. Humiliation cannot touch the master because he is a free man whom no one on earth can embarrass. In any circumstances, you can have the attitude of a master.

Your mind is a faithful servant but a bad master. If you let your mind do whatever it wants, you do not have the attitude of the master. You act as a slave. Do not let your emotions take control of you. Many of us have a heap of negative emotions within us such as fear, hate, jealousy and envy which consume our mind. Such thoughts are toxic.

A negative emotion enters stealthily into our minds like a thief at night in an unguarded house. Many times, it enters the house in broad daylight as a guest. Then, it becomes a host, and, finally, a master. The guest, who was supposed to respect the master's rules at his home, has silenced the master. He is now giving orders in the master's place. In the same way, your mind, which is supposed to be your servant, will take away your power and enslave you. Give orders to your mind as a master. When you have the attitude of a master toward your mind, then you are the master of your destiny.

Waste No Time on Negative Thinking
Do not waste your time on toxic feelings that pollute your heart. The pendulum swings marking the passage of time calmly and precisely. You will never be able to get back the time you have wasted. One day, you will wake up from your sleep and you will be short of time to accomplish anything valuable because you have not much longer left to live. Just think! If you had known in advance that was going to happen to you, what would you have done differently with your life?

You have planned too many things to achieve in the future. You may intend to spend your next holiday in Katmandu, to triple the income of your business, or to buy a new house. Suddenly, all these things become irrelevant. Other things that you have never thought about come into your consciousness. What occupied your attention before is no longer important now.

One's awareness of the passage of time is a responsible attitude. Energy should not be wasted. Instead, be very conscious of where you are expending your energy. Do not waste it chasing unnecessary things. If you have wasted all your fuel in collecting shells, you will not have any strength to dig when you know where the treasure is hidden.

The mind is like a monkey. The monkey swings from one branch to another. Our mind is like that restless monkey. Controlling the mind is an arduous task. Rather, change your attitude. Give your mind the right orders as you would command a servant. Be the master of your mind and use it with awareness.

Your Faithful Servant

Do not Bite; Just Shine

Both a good attitude and a negative attitude come from the same energy. The only difference is direction. Use your mind to become who you want to be.

The mosquito and the glow-worm are both small. But their instincts are different. As small as it might be, the mosquito is powerful. It can suck your blood. In India, when a swarm of mosquitos is around, it is a real struggle to cope with them. It does not miss its target even in the dark. It hums in your ear. Its bites ruin your sleep. When you hit the mosquito, it dies after sucking a tiny bit of your blood and leaving an itchy red bump on your skin.

My parents used to talk on the veranda, while we kids attempted to catch glow-worms. In the darkness of the night, the small worm was luminous. For me it was like holding a star in my hand. Unlike the mosquito, the glow-worm provides light. It makes people happy when they see it.

You can choose your attitude. You can bite or shine. Instead of draining the energy from people as the mosquito does, your attitude can be like a glow-worm that shines and lights its little lantern. It is easy to be like a mosquito but it requires a conscious effort to be like a glow-worm.

Your Well is not the Ocean

Both temple and church were built to give us an atmosphere of purity and divinity. The church is a quiet place apart from the hustle and bustle of the outside world. I was in a catholic church in Paris one afternoon when the church was empty. I appreciated the calmness of the place and I felt relaxed.

I was in prayer in front of the infant Jesus in the arms of the Mother Mary when a man came in with his wife. The couple sat on the bench before me on my right side. The man turned back. He was staring at me. He looked angry. I was embarrassed as I did not understand his attitude. The man asked his wife, "Why is this lady here? She is not even from our country."

The Attitude of the Masters *by Céline Théron*

I was surprised by his words, for the man had come to pray to Christ, who was not from his country either. Our narrow-minded attitude is like a well. How can we recognize the master, Jesus-Christ, who is like an ocean if we are sitting in a narrow-minded well?

Come out of your well to see how vast the ocean is. The source of the well is the ocean. Even if you are a drop in the ocean, you are part of it. Hence, you are the ocean, too. As the rivers and streams finally find their way to the ocean, your ultimate growth is to become one with the ocean known as "the Infinite."

Do not put any limitations on yourself. Our nature is infinite. But, to be aware of it, you have to be open. At the seashore, merchants sell all kinds of beautiful shells. People hold a shell at their ears and listen to the sound of the sea while the waves lap at their feet. When you can enjoy the sound of the vast ocean, why would you limit your experience to the shell's echo?

You get from the ocean what you want, which is either a vast or a tiny amount of water. In the same way, in life you get what you think you deserve. Expand yourself. Be open to all life has to offer.

Many worlds revolve around you. Discover all the richness and diversity with an open-minded attitude. We are confined in our mind. Prejudice is bondage. A narrow-minded attitude encloses you in its circle like the snake that devours its own tail. We are living in a closed house. Open the window. Let the air and the sun's rays enter into your home.

Free yourself from a narrow-minded attitude, and you will feel that you are the master. Then, everything will appear to you as vast as the ocean. But for many, life is far from being an ocean. Without an open attitude, your mind drives you into madness.

They Called Him the "Mad Man"

In the countryside where I lived in India, women and men

frequently passed by in the streets selling all kinds of things such as prepared foods, sweets, *sarees* and bracelets as they went from house to house. Some peasants raised ducks to sell them. They attached thread to groups of three ducks each so that they could not move. They then put them in a basket which they carried on their head as they went through the villages selling ducks.

In my village, there was a man called "mad man" because he was violent. He hit his wife and attacked people. He behaved as if he had lost his mind. But he was not really mad. He was a fairly prosperous man who deliberately mistreated people. The mad man failed to have the attitude of the masters.

I used to play on the large balcony of my house. One afternoon I was watching from the balcony a peasant with his basket of ducks on his head as he passed by my house. He stopped in front of the so-called mad man's house to sell his ducks. The mad man came out. He grabbed the basket, seized the ducks, and cut their throats. He then knocked the poor peasant onto the ground and kicked the man in the stomach. The poor merchant cried hopelessly. When the mad man stopped hitting him, the merchant begged at his feet. He said with tears pouring down his face, "Please sir, have mercy! Pay me for those ducks. If I return home this evening without any money, my children and wife will not have anything to eat." The mad man just kicked him again and went back into his home. He slammed the door behind him as he entered. The poor merchant stayed on the ground with one hand on his head, sobbing.

I quivered in fear after seeing this. My spirit rebelled against the injustice the mad man had meted out on the duck merchant. I felt warm tears run slowly down my cheeks, for what could a child do in that situation but cry? I felt as hopeless as the merchant. After many years, a person went back to the village and reported that the man who was called mad man had become truly mad. He finally had lost his mind,

The Attitude of the Masters *by Céline Théron*

wasted all his money, and was now living as a beggar.

This is the Law of Karma. Whatever you do, it will be returned to you. You can hide the seed under the earth, but it will one day sprout. Whatever negative emotion you hold in a secret place in your mind will come to light eventually.

Negative emotions do more harm to you than to your enemies. Emotions are like your possessions. Your entire possessions do not have the same quality. For instance, your shoes and your cigarette both belong to you. But they offer a different quality of services. Your shoes you are using to protect your feet while your cigarette is using *you* because it destroys your health. Negative emotions use you from inside and lead to your downfall. But this does not mean that you have to ignore your emotions.

Be True to Your Emotions

Have an authentic attitude. Conventional wisdom has taught us from a very young age to control our natural emotions. From boyhood, men have been told, "Don't cry like a girl!" Often, men are also not allowed to laugh. Men are expected to be serious. What kind of life is for a man when he can neither cry nor laugh? When you feel compassion upon seeing the tears of a helpless person you will be reproached for being too sensitive. To be hard as a rock is the easy way. However, having a gentle spirit gives you strong spiritual strength.

Allow natural emotions. Do not force nature in any direction. Natural emotions make you human. You do not need to see a specialist if you have lost a dear one. Grief is natural in this situation, but we are not always allowed to express our emotions. If you cry a little loudly, that means you are uncivilized. You have to hold your emotion inside and cry soundlessly even at the death of your dearest loved one. What is the use of being civilized and having manners that prevent you from being human?

Do not adopt a false attitude. The actor on the movie screen expresses such emotions as love, anger, and hatred without feeling them. But in life you live your emotions. Do not act as if you do not feel them. If you are sad, accept it. Do not go about saying you are fine with the idea of being positive. It is hard to pretend not being sad when you are. The truth will tear the veil of your false laugher from your face and reveal the tears you shed. When you act as if you do not feel an emotion, it divides you. The mind of man cannot be split. Be true to your emotions. It is the way to have harmony inside you.

Laughter is a good healer. It is scientifically proved that, even if your laughter is false, you can still get good benefits from it. However, a false smile can be a good exercise for your lips, not for your heart. You cannot feel the joy of hearty laughter if you try to fake it. Every time you try to make real something false, you will be deceived.

Sometime, you might feel anger, envy or jealousy. Do not let your self-esteem allow you to hide these emotions. For instance, if you deny that you can have anger, and then, someone insults you, suddenly, you are a different person. There is divinity inside all creatures. To gain that divinity, you first have to accept your humanity with all its weakness and strength. You can lose that divinity by being false.

You can't escape from your real emotions. They are sleeping silently but can wake up with vigor at any time.

I once saw a lake full of lotus flowers. I approached the water to pluck one. My driver rushed up and stopped me. He said, "Be careful. There are crocodiles." The water was still and silent like the moon. The beautiful white lotus flowers decorated it. No one could imagine that inside this beauty, dangerous crocodiles were living. Similarly, in human beings, we can sometimes find a dormant animal. It can wake up in some circumstances. The tiger roaring within is hiding to better jump on his prey.

You are More than Just Emotions

If you try to get rid of all your negative emotions, you need many lives. Have you ever seen a flock of crows pecking at grains? If you throw one stone at the crows, all will fly at once. In the same way, awareness is like a stone that makes negative emotions disappear. The same serpent that injects the venom can suck it back. Likewise, you create your negative emotions. You can also use your awareness to get rid of them.

Have the attitude of a watcher. Do not judge yourself by your weakness or strength. Be a witness to your emotions. Buddha calls this *mindfulness*. Watch with awareness what is happening inside you. The simple method is not to be identified with your emotions. Awareness is a transforming force. If you feel in rage that you want to slap someone, watch yourself, and be aware that you are carrying the strong emotion of anger. If you feel hatred, be aware of it. It will dissipate. The more you are aware of your negative emotions, the quicker they will disappear.

Have an aloof attitude toward your emotions. Have you noticed that you are often a good advisor and an efficient problem solver for somebody else but not for yourself? You are efficient because you are a third person watching the problem with a certain degree of objectivity. It gives you the strength to say to you neighbour who has lost her child, "Death happens to everybody. Even if you weep thousands of years, it will not bring your son back." But when the same tragedy happens in your life, you lose all control. Now, you are one with your problem. Keep distance from your negative emotion. Be the watcher. The negative emotions will fade away. Also learn to respond instead of react in order to be in control of your emotions.

Respond Instead of Reacting

Most of time, we react to what happens to us. Someone gives you a blow. The normal attitude is to want to hit him back. Your reaction in anger is an unconscious attitude. You regret what you have done when you are conscious of your attitude. When you react, you are not acting. You just answered impulsively to the provocation of the man who has become your master. You are not in control of yourself. The attitude of the master is not to react but to respond.

During a festival in Durga temple in my village, people were sitting around gossiping. I was sitting in the midst of them. Some Indian people—especially elderly people—after their meal used to take a few slices of the nut wrapped in a betel leaf along with white lime. The entire mixture is then placed in the mouth and chewed, which produces a flow of bright red juice. They then spit the juice into a pot used for this purpose.

I chewed on the wrapped betel leaf. It was a complex art to chew it. It was difficult for me to keep all the juice in my mouth and continue chewing. A person next to me said something funny. I suddenly laughed. I spat the juice involuntary on a lady who had come from a far off village to accompany the impoverished who came to the festival from there. Her face was now covered with blood-red juice. Nobody said anything to me because they considered me wealthy. Everybody was looking at the lady. It was a disgrace for her. But the lady was as calm as before.

I told her, "Sorry, sister!"

She cleaned her face with her *saree*. She affectionately said in a soft voice, "Don't worry!" The lady's generous smile warmed my heart. I was grateful to her. The lady responded to the situation with her feminine tenderness. Despite the embarrassing situation, she did not react but responded with kindness and understanding. Her attitude revealed her inner strength and lofty nature. She had the attitude of a master.

Do not let anyone affect you. If someone insults you and you reply with insults, you dot have the attitude of the master. You become the puppet of the man. When anger or hatred arises, halt a moment. It will help you not to react impulsively. After a silence, you can respond fully conscious of your attitude.

The Attitude of the Masters *by Céline Théron*

Retrain Your Mind to See the Good in Others

Our natural tendency seems to remember more bitter memories than beautiful moments. You may have done many good things to people. But, if you have done one unfavorable thing, some of them will remember it their whole lives, and they will not miss an opportunity to pay you back. They live in anger and hatred, dreaming of revenge. The attitude of vengeance is capable of destroying everything. Yet, it is powerless to build up anything with it. Hatred is a dreadful attitude. It is a poison that kills you first before your enemy. Do not fill your mind with bitterness and turn your goodness to filth. When the time comes where you give up the life of hatred, vengeance and violence, you are a new master.

You will not cultivate negative emotions if you see the good side of a person. I could never forget my first encounter with the *Tzigane* in the French countryside where I once lived. The *Tzigane* are originally from India. The *Tzigane* reminded me of the tribal people from my village. I could see the *Tzigane* in a caravan. They looked very poor. My eldest sister, Claudine, gave me some money and said, "Give this money to these people." They were surprised when I approached them without fear.

Later in the evening, my sister Claudine and I took bags of food, and clothes to the *Tzigane*. There were young men, ladies, elderly people, and kids. It was almost a village. I told them, "These are for you." They were happy.

An old woman approached us. She said, "Please, take this painting." She offered us the painting, *The Milkmaid*. It was a beautiful painting of a housemaid in a plain room carefully pouring milk into an earthenware pot on a table.

During their stay, we met the *Tzigane* many times. They loved us as their family members. People, who had seen us meeting the *Tzigane*, warned us how dangerous these people are. They said, "They are wandering people. They steal and even kill. Do not approach them!"

The next season, the *Tzigane* came back to camp in the

same place. They looked at me when I passed by. I still remember the sad eyes of those young people when they saw me avoiding them. I was sad, too. However, I was afraid to approach them. I had been alone with them many times. They had done no harm to me. Now I feared these same people because I had more knowledge of who they were, and I was looking at their negative side.

The *Tzigane* are put apart from the rest of society. The truth is these people had goodness and something special in them. They were people with great values such as love, solidarity and authenticity. I still remember how separation from them deeply hurt me.

When we look at the good side of things, we realize that, in reality, we belong to the same community that is called "humanity."

We often have a judgmental attitude. Someone's bad attitude annoys us. One stumbles more than another. He who stumbles more, we call "bad"; he who stumbles less, we call "good." Good and bad are not two different things. They are one and the same energy. The difference is not one of kind, but of degree.

Try to find good in people. It is hard to find a person who has nothing good in him or her. Just make a slight change in your thinking and attitude and look at what is positive in people. It will make a big difference in your life. Some people are like jackfruit. Its outside has the appearance of a blunt thorn. Its surface is sticky latex. You have to oil your hands to avoid the sticky milk. Once you open the fruit, the interior is full of goodness. You will find sweet orange-yellow bulbs to eat. The tastiness of fruit deserves the effort you took. So it is with some people. You should not judge them from their appearance. You might miss a beautiful soul such as of Socrates behind their ugly outward appearance.

Do you know the difference between the winnow and the sieve? A sieve allows all the good things to pass through its pores while retaining the chaff materials within. A winnow, on the other hand, blows away the useless stuff and in the end retains only good grains. You can decide to be a sieve or a winnow. You can choose a negative attitude and spoil your life by holding onto only bad things. Or, you can choose a positive attitude and retain all beautiful things that are happening to you and around you. Your mind is a faithful servant. You can use it as a sieve or a winnow. Your mind gives you alternatives: "This is good. This is bad." But, you are the master. You choose your attitude. So, whenever there is an alternative, lean towards the good side.

Purify your thoughts, and you will see goodness. Before one whose mind and thoughts are pure, even wild beasts will bow at his feet. When your mind is positive you know that everyone is part of you. That is why Gandhi worried for the soldier who kicked him. You feel one with the universe. That's why Buddha once halted for a long time on his path to let a colony of ants pass by. Buddha was connected with all living beings, human, animal, and vegetable. The masters feel one with the universe.

The Universe is Not Separate from You

Human beings are not strangers to one another. There is interdependence, a subtle relation between people. Each individual is a part of the universe. There are moments when every man feels that he is one with the universe and thus he feels infinite. Therefore, in doing harm to his neighbour, the individual hurts himself. Once you understand this, the attitudes of jealousy, hatred, and all kinds of bad intentions will disappear because you can now truthfully ask: "To whom can I express my bad emotions but to myself?"

The attitude of the oneness with the universe is conveyed through love and sympathy toward our neighbours. The nature of man wants to help his fellow human beings. People are like that.

Once I saw a baby in a bus. He wept to get a piece of bread from his mom. When his mother gave him a slice of bread, before eating it, the baby extended the bread to his mother's mouth. She did not want. So he held the bread to strangers in the bus. When people shook their heads and said no with a smile, the baby finally ate the bread. But he first offered to others something he had cried to have. The baby boy had instantly and naturally the attitude of a master who first cares for others.

People have proven that they are able to love not only those who are close to them but also those who are far away, in other lands. When huge waves of the ocean swallowed kids, women, men, animals, all countries felt love for those who had suffered this catastrophe as they did for people near to their hearts. Even without knowing those who perished, they shared their pain as friends. It is like if you hurt your foot, your eyes cry. In the same way, we are all connected.

The person who denies this interdependence and thinks being separated from others goes upstream, swimming against the current in life. Man is not an island. Each individual soul is a piece of the universal soul. The masters feel one with the universe.

Allow the Sun to Stimulate Your Mind

The sun rises for everybody. *Surya* (sun) is light. It is a symbol of God that gives life to all living creatures. To allow the sun stimulate our mind is to allow God to light our being. My mother used to offer prayer with *bhakti* (devotion) to the sun. It was a sacred moment. I learned the *Surya Namaskar* (Sun Salutation) from my mother. In Kanyakumari, I was with hundreds people early in the morning waiting for the sun. It was still dark. The sun majestically appeared. We welcomed it with joy.

It is meditative to share the morning silence of the sun rising. You have to learn how to get energy from the sun. Let the sunlight enter your being. You will feel a new energy. You will feel more alive. Darkness and light cannot exist together. The darkness fades in the face of the sun. Similarly, to be

The Attitude of the Masters *by Céline Théron*

unconquered by darkness and keep your attitude positive, turn your mind to the sun. The attitude of the master is grandiose like the sun. Their mind is always turned toward light.

Have you ever observed the sunflower? In the early morning when the sun is rising, the flower opens its petals to the touch of light, as it faces towards the sunrise. Each day, it follows the whole journey of the sun. By evening, when the sun declines, the flower closes its petals again. Be like the sunflower and always face your mind towards the sun. Let its light illuminate your whole being. You will get a powerful energy from the sun. Allow the sun to stimulate your mind. It will have a positive impact on your attitude.

CHAPTER FIVE

You Are the Positive Force

You Are the Positive Force

~~~≫○◯○≪~~~

The sun had risen. The haze was moving and the sky was clear. A crowd had gathered on the mountain and a voice resounded — it was the voice of Jesus of Nazareth. He said, "Look at the birds in the sky! They do not plant or harvest. They do not even store grain in barns, and yet God feeds them. How much more worth are you than the birds?"

The master Jesus saw people broken in heart. He felt an overwhelming pity for Man. He was a sower. He sowed the seeds of hope, faith and love so that humanity might reap the harvest. He embraced the earth without discrimination between people. The fishermen, lepers, prostitutes and thieves, all felt great in his presence. He took the stone that was rejected by the builders and made it the cornerstone.

That is the positive attitude of a master with whom contact will transform a man to his very roots. Whoever comes into contact with you, make sure they go back energized, purified, inspired and transformed. You are the positive force that transforms everything you touch.

The Attitude of the Masters *by Céline Théron*

You cannot be a positive force while living in the surface. "I sit on a man's back choking him and making him carry me. I am very sorry for him and wish to ease his lot by all possible means; except by getting off his back." This statement by Leo Tolstoy holds some truth. The positive attitude is not merely wishing good to others. Your positive attitude should manifest from your being. Our being is greater and deeper than our behavior, words or actions.

In the modern world, we are afraid of depth. People expect transformation without any change in their thoughts, lifestyle and attitude. None of the people seem to have either the time or the desire to attempt to change the state of their being. Without a transformation in the depths of our being, the positive attitude can be only a shadow, not a reality. The positive seeds are already sown; the sprouts are waiting to come out of the earth.

Nurture the Positive Seeds within You

I have seen parents in India beating their sons with a broom which consists of bundles of reeds when they did something wrong, but the punishment was out of love. It was not given with enmity. The parents wanted their children to have a positive attitude. They chose a hard task to teach a person to be good. The kids who went through this punishment always said later, "At that time I thought I was being treated very harshly, but now I am full of gratefulness towards those people who were hard on me. They awakened some dormant strength in me." The good seed sown in childhood was not sown in vain.

My childhood playground in India was nature. I played the old traditional Indian game with stones. In this game, stones are usually tossed into the air and you should not drop the stone you tossed up and not touch other stones while picking up the ones you cast into the air. I also played with dragonflies, and took care of a baby crow. Life was simple, wild, and natural.

You Are the Positive Force

When I came to France, I was put into contact with toys for the first time. In my primary school, there was a playroom full of all kinds of them. We always had play time before going to the classroom. One day, I took a liking to one of those toys so much that I did not want to put back. I wanted to take it at home. During recreation, I showed my favorite toy to my sister Aline and said, "Do you see? It is a nice toy. I'm going to keep it at home." My sister got very angry and told me sternly, "Go and put this toy back immediately. If not, I'll go straight away to inform your teacher!" This strong warning frightened me. I thought at that time she was being very hard. But today I admire the wisdom of my sister. Although a kid, she taught a great lesson in my life, which was to not desire something that does not belong to me.

The seed of the positive attitude is sown by the past in the tender soul of a child. Parents, teachers or gurus have spread seeds of positive attitudes earlier in our life.

Here is another story from my school days. In my private high school in France, some of the students were violent. They were sent back from their previous school because of their bad attitude. They came to school drunk. They broke chairs and tore up the window curtains in the classrooms.

These students chose me as their target because I was very calm. They were very mischievous with me. However, I did not complain about them to the principal because they were my classmates. But a boy from my class did it for me. He went to see the principal of the school and informed him about the students' attitude toward me. The principal gave them a severe warning. But even after that incident, I continued to have problems with them, especially with one of the teenagers named Caroline who was the leader of the group.

I was very anxious to go to the school, but I did not know what to do about Caroline and her friends. I finally sat down and talked with Caroline. I explained to her that I was suffering because of their attitude to the point I could not concentrate on my studies. I asked her to help me by not doing any more harm to me. She attentively listened and then said, "All right. I'll stop!" I told her, "If you really mean it, then promise me." She promised to never bother me again. Every time she wanted to do something wrong to me, I reminded her of her promise. I still remember how hard she fought against herself to keep her word. Even this violent teenager finally learned that one should not break his or her promise.

As the roots of the tree are hidden in the earth, so are the seeds of positivity hidden within you. The banyan tree which covers acres of ground sprouted from a little seed. You are as mighty as the banyan tree with all the positive force you have within you, so allow yourself to grow as large spiritually as a banyan tree.

Be Like an Alchemist

Doctors sometimes advise their patients to take rest in a mountain climate for the improvement of their health. The change of climate is beneficial not only for your health but also for your mind.

I was once in Ooty, in India. There was serenity and calmness in this city with all its lofty mountains, great lakes, *nilgiri* trees and beautiful flower gardens. The climate of the Pyrenees in France has also a special atmosphere that erases all stress.

Man's soul is transformed according to the climate in which he lives, or the company he keeps. The transformation is almost magnetic. Magnets attract iron due to the influence of their magnetic field upon it. The iron that is exposed to a strong magnet becomes magnetic itself afterward. When you have a positive attitude that is positively magnetic, people around you are bound to become positive too. When you are close to a successful person, you will aim to do your best to become successful.

Suppose you love a hero, an actor, or a person that you appreciate. You will consciously or unconsciously try to have the same attitude as him and absorb some of his qualities.

You Are the Positive Force

When you shine as a sun, the person at your side is also lighted. The moon is not the source of its light. That light is not coming from the moon. It comes from the sun. The sunlight falls on the moon and the rays are reflected back, and those reflected rays are visible to our eyes. When you shine as a sun, your light reflects on the person at your side and she will shine as the moon. Your positive attitude can even change someone else's life.

That Little Thing We Call Encouragement

You are the positive force. With just a word of encouragement you can make magic happen in someone's life. Discouragement seems to be meaningless, but it can demoralize even a determined person. Many people give up because of discouragement. Their failures and frustrations push them to quit. As a result, they take no more actions.

Encouragement is powerful. In the environment I was born into, people did not wait for someone to encourage them. They found themselves encouragement through many odd things. Hearing the house lizards' 'tik-tik-tik' gave them a new energy. It was a good omen. My mother felt encouraged hearing the crow crowing. In our garden, a crow with only one foot used to visit us. Mama believed in the prediction of that crow. When my dad was in France, she said, "Every time this crow crows, you are going to receive a letter from your dad." Hardly did she finish saying that then the postman was at the door with a letter from my dad in hand.

If a lizard or a crow can encourage people, we can do more. The masters are great motivators. They give hope for others. You can dissipate someone's weariness by your encouragement. The faded flower blossoms as if life is given back when you water it. So it is that with a word of encouragement, you can awaken a tired man's positive force.

In my village, the parrot fortune teller was a great motivator. Parrot fortune-telling is a type of astrology. It involves using green parakeets which are trained to pick up fortune cards.

The Attitude of the Masters *by Céline Théron*

A parrot fortune teller typically sits beneath a tree or by the side of the road. He has a cage which contains a parrot. The cards are either spread out or stacked in front of him. Each card contains the image of a Hindu deity and some cards contain images of Jesus or Buddha.

When you sit before him, he opens the cage and lets the parrot out. He often calls it by its name. He instructs the parrot to pick a card for you. The parrot walks over to the cards, picks one from the stack or the spread with its beak and gives it to the teller. The fortune teller opens the card, and based on the image tells you your fortune. It is usually good news. For instance, a good job is waiting for you, you are going to get married or you will travel to a foreign land.

He always walked through the village streets with his caged parrot and we always gathered around him. Each word of his good predictions always had a positive impact on us. Indian people as well as tourists loved to hear his good predictions. The man's positive words put a smile on their face and for a few pennies they were motivated. I was also happy after his simple encouragement. Adopt the positive attitude of the motivator, and boost the energy in people with your positive words.

Learning to drive was almost an impossible thing for me. I was so scared of driving. Once I turned the key, I imagined all kind of dangers: a child running just in front of my car, another vehicle coming along the wrong side of the road, or my car hitting a tree. The driving instructors were always yelling at me and claimed that I would never get the license. They finally told me that I had failed so many times that I only had one more chance before I had to start the procedure all over again.

I had already lost all hope that I would get my license by the time of my final test. The inspector shook my hand and said two encouraging words to me: "Good driving!"

My hand trembled while I turned the key. I had hardly driven for a few minutes before I became very nervous when

You Are the Positive Force

I saw a group of youths crossing the road ahead of us. The inspector had the reputation that he would never forgive you if you made mistakes involving the walkers.

The young people came close to my car and circled it. I did not know how to get out of the crowd. I gave up. The youths looked at me, smiled, and then clasped their hands with joy to encourage me. Suddenly, everything changed. Their enthusiasm and energy were contagious. I felt confident that this time I would get the license, and I did.

A word or a sign of encouragement is enough to help a person to go ahead. However, motivation or encouragement has a positive effect on someone for a moment whereas inspiration has a lasting impact. Inspire others and bring a new breeze into their life.

Inspiration is Divine

Inspire people by your positive attitude. Inspiration is a divine call that wakes up the soul. It transforms ordinary people into extraordinary. Inspiration once transformed a lawyer into a great spiritual master. In the beginning, Mohandas Gandhi was an advocate but then he was inspired by King Harishchandra. That changed his destiny and also the history of his country.

The life of the great King Harishchandra is engraved in the mind of many Indian people. In our conversation, we often refer to his name when it is a question of truth. Harishchandra vowed to remain truthful at all times. He successfully faced the severe ordeals created by Vishwamitra. In the realm of truthfulness, he sacrificed everything he had, including his kingdom, and even his wife and son. He took work as a grave-guardian.

This story of Harishchandra showed the path of truth to Gandhi. Harishchandra had led a fateful life in order to remain truthful. Knowing his life, many people would be afraid to follow the narrow and dangerous path of truth. But the play *Harishchandra* captured Gandhi's heart. Gandhi said, "Why should not all be truthful like Harishchandra? This was the question I asked myself day and night. To follow truth and to go through all the ordeals Harishchandra went through was the one ideal it inspired in me."

That inspiration was a divine call that transformed a simple man into *Mahatma*, a great soul. Gandhi experimented with *Satyam* (truth). He proved to the world that a single voice of the man who speaks *Satyam* is much more powerful than the power of an entire empire. His belief in *Satyam* and *Ahimsa* (non-violence) brought the freedom of India from the British Empire. He became in his turn a great inspiration for the world. Look at the life of the masters and take inspiration from them. The people who can inspire you can be your parents, your friend, or a stranger you met in the streets. Look deeply into your life and see how you can inspire others in turn and wake up in them their sleeping power. Through your inspiration, help people to hear the divine call to become the kind of person they are born to be.

CHAPTER SIX

There is Wisdom in Your Suffering

There is Wisdom in Your Suffering

―――❁―――

Many years ago, I watched a movie. I remember just one scene. God was angry against the people of Sodom and Gomorrah. He decided to destroy those cities. He allowed a man named Lot to take his family and flee into the mountains. He warned Lot, "Do not look back!" Once they were out of the city, a rain of fire descended upon it. Lot's wife heard the devastating sounds of fire and brimstone. She looked back behind her, and she was changed into a pillar of salt.

Never Look Back

To me, this story shows how challenging it is for us to not look back. Lot's wife had left her home, and maybe her friends; and everything was now in flame. She could not resist looking back.

What happened to us in our pasts is a part of our life. The past lingers with us in the form of our memories of joy and pain. The common attitude is to look back. However, the past does not exist anymore. If you remain stuck in your past, it will turn you into a pillar, which is dead stone. The past is dead. We can't get life from it.

We can look to the past and learn from it. Did you hear about the lion's retrospection? The lion in the forest has the instinct of looking back on the path already walked. Like the lion, you can have a self-analysis and a review of the past in order to learn from your experiences.

Your attitude toward your past determines the quality of your present moment. You cannot live fully the present while thinking about the past. You need a great courage to let go of the past and come to the present. How long have you been reliving your past? Find out what makes you cling to it. Sometimes the past becomes an obsession, difficult to get rid of because you bear a heavy weight in your heart that's called "guilt."

Forgive Me Damy, My Friend

I heard about a teenager who had a serious argument with his uncle. In his anger he said, "When I come back, I do not want to see you at home." He slammed the door and went out. When he returned home late in the evening, he was told, "Your uncle is dead." The young boy cried, saying, "My words became true. I can't see my uncle anymore." That feeling of guilt followed him ever since. He regretted his harsh words against his uncle. He could not forgive himself even after so many years. But it had been a cruel coincidence that his uncle had died while he was out that day. His angry words did not kill his uncle.

Our conscience is our inner judge that condemns us. I know from my experience how hard it is to get rid of the feeling of guilt. I have many memories of my friend and dog, Damy. He may just be a dog to others, but for me he is a friend forever. I can never forget him. I was just a child when I left my home country. The separation from my dearest friend Damy was very painful.

I still remember the day I left India. It was night and I could see only the light coming from my house. I was sitting

There is Wisdom in Your Suffering

in the car. Damy was on the doorstep looking around with sad eyes. At that young age, I could not understand that he would feel abandoned. He walked around the car and approached each person carrying luggage. He expected someone to acknowledge him while feeling instinctively that his family was leaving.

Damy was a loyal companion and a devoted servant that I regret having lost. I was an isolated child. In fact, other children did not play with me because they said that I was different from them. Therefore, I am grateful to Damy because he was my only childhood friend and a kind of "big brother" to me too.

Although we had been very close and we played together a lot, I remember I made him suffer once. It happened the day someone had offered me a little dog which I brought home. I played with the new dog. I washed it and gave it milk to drink. All the while, Damy watched all these scenes from the refuge he had taken in a corner outside the house. Subsequently, he did not nourish himself anymore and he became very ill. In this case, he suffered in silence. For this reason I gave back the little dog.

"I was only a child, unaware of your pain, Damy. I regret it today!" I sometimes think.

Damy occupied many roles at home and the main one consisted of being a guardian. His gratitude toward his master, my father, was infinite. He acted as my dad's bodyguard and followed him everywhere he went. Once, while my dad was watching over the fields, some men suddenly attacked him. Witnessing this scene, Damy ran from a long distance to warn us. Thanks to him, we were able to rescue my dad. I thank him for all his good acts. I ask Damy's forgiveness for not being able to return the same to him.

Today when I look back at that part of my past, I always feel pain in my heart. I share the suffering of my dog that felt abandoned by people he loved and served. He was there for me when I was alone as a child, and I was powerless to bring him with me when I left home. I could not be there to help him when the neighbor's to whom my parents entrusted Damy to watch over did not take care of him. Nor was I there when he died. I did not know when I left the country that I would never see him again.

"Forgive me my friend!" I often silently say to Damy. I would do anything in my power to erase the suffering caused to him, but there is nothing I can do now. The only thing I can do is ask for his forgiveness.

Get Over Your Guilt

If you carry a strong feeling about something that happened in the past, release yourself from it. If you have offended anyone, show a humble attitude by asking forgiveness. If you have done something wrong, try to solve it. If nothing can be done about what happened, accept it, make the strong decision to never take that wrong road again, and move on.

Your attitude toward guilt is relevant. You can turn your feelings of guilt into a positive transformational force. Your heart is filled with remorse, and your tears cleanse it. Now, you are a new person. You come out of guilt more experienced and wiser. Believe me, until you free yourself from your guilt you cannot live in the present. Your attitude of constantly condemning yourself will not help you. If you drop your feelings of guilt, your spirit will feel refreshed. Then your growth and emotional stability are possible for you because, by letting go of your guilt, you have cut it as surely as Alexander cut the Gordian Knot in the Temple of Zeus.

Make This Line Shorter

My sister invited an American young lady to our home. I was in my room at first as they sat laughing in the living room. I finally joined them because I was curious to meet my sister's friend. I discovered that she was entertaining my sister with all kinds of games. She was happy to see me. She invited me to participate in their games.

There is Wisdom in Your Suffering

She drew a line on a piece of paper. She asked me, "How can you make this line shorter without touching it?" I thought about it for a while, but no solution came to my mind. I grew impatient to know the answer. Finally, our visitor drew another line that was much longer horizontally on the paper a few inches above the one she had previously drawn.

"Now," she asked, "Hasn't the first line become shorter in comparison to the newer, longer line?"

"Yes, you are right," I replied. "How smart you are!"

It was just a game at that time, but later these two lines, one shorter and another longer, was a great lesson in my life.

Mama offered me a Pyrenean Mountain Dog. We called her Damy in the memory of my friend Damy in India whom I talked about earlier in this chapter. I was holding Damy's face in my hands when she closed her eyes for the last time the day she died. It was a painful moment for me. I could not concentrate on anything else afterwards because I kept thinking about Damy. One month later, I lost my Mama; now a bigger other line than the first one was drawn for me. I forgot the first problem because now I was affected by something bigger that shuttered my whole life.

The masters know how to make a line shorter. They learned to see a situation through contrast. We sometimes need contrast in our lives to apprehend an issue. We need contrast to appreciate or feel better about a situation.

Life can seem to be a burden while focusing only on our issues. We need contrast. Raise your eyes and look at your neighbors struggles, and you will feel light. Your attitude of gratitude can diminish your worries. When you look at your life with gratitude, you will discover how fortunate you are while many others are going through even worse difficulties than yours.

Do you know someone who is going through a tougher situation than you are? Maybe that person is in your family, in your workplace, or in the home next door to yours. Find a bigger line somewhere that makes your own line shorter.

Look upon an innocent orphan abandoned in the streets; it will make the line shorter. Look at the poor people who toil like animals for a handful of rice; it will make the line shorter. Look at the helpless widows shivering with fear for her child; it will make the line shorter. Our line is not always the biggest one.

Life Is a Mystery
I've always wondered about the mystery of life. Two flowers blossom on the same branch, but one flower decorates the champion's stage, the marriage's celebration hall, the house, and a lady's hair. The other beautiful flower is used for a garland decorating a dead person, thrown away on a sidewalk, or trampled underfoot by people.

Like these flowers, some people know happiness, others pain. We have all asked at least once in our lives the question: "Why is this happening to me?" The eternal question is "Why?" Life has its own logic that cannot be understood by us, because life is mysterious. Everything to it has a hidden secret. African tribes worship the serpent because it is always in contact with the Mother Earth. Its whole body touches the ground and it must, therefore, know all the earth's secrets. In the same way, when you have to suffer for a while, life will reveal to you its secrets.

Do you go through great challenges? Do you not know why all this is happening to you? Have no fear of the reason why for, sooner or later, the secret will be revealed to you. You will then see the solution to your problems.

Life is your greatest teacher, but it is a different type of teacher. It does not give you an examination after having taught you the lesson. On the contrary, it first put you to a test, and then it taught you the lesson.

One who has not suffered does not know what life is all about. Once I talked to a man who confided to me, "I'll tell you a secret: I have never been sad in my life!" At that time, I thought that he was the luckiest person in the world. Now,

There is Wisdom in Your Suffering

I understand that he had missed something in his life. Life is meant to be lived fully. How can you know happiness if you have not also known pain? If you want to ascend to the skies, you also have to descend into the abyss.

The Messenger of Misery

Marlon Brando, the famous Hollywood actor, endured a personal tragedy when his son was convicted of murder. "The messenger of misery has visited my house." He lamented after the verdict. Your wealth, prestige, fame or virtues cannot block the path of this messenger. He will visit your house at least once in your life.

It is said that once upon a time in India, kings never killed the messenger even if he was an enemy. Have the attitude of those kings, ready to receive the messenger without hostility. Do not try to kill him because you do not like the message. Your attitude to receive him as a guest will change everything. Once the messenger visits you, often he will not leave you so soon. But he knows that he is a guest and he is not supposed to stay in your house permanently. One day, he will leave you and your house. Misery in life is a guest. Suffering is not permanent.

Have a strong attitude when you face problems. Do not lose heart because you are going through unbearable pain. It is a sign that the end is near. There is a saying in India that before disappearing, the flame burns brightest. So it is with pain and suffering.

Deep Wound – Profound Transformation

All the blows you received create a great change in your attitude. They touch your soul and transform your being. The gold shines the brightest once passed through the furnace. The stone which bears the hammering of the chisel is transformed into a beautiful statue. Similarly, once you have gone through harsh ordeals, you are like the material ready in the hand of the Maker to accomplish great things. Great changes

The Attitude of the Masters *by Céline Théron*

happened in an individual's life or in nations by the masters who went through fateful experience. Deep wound causes profound transformation. You become stronger.

I was impressed by the story of Raja Ram Mohan Roy (or Ram Mohan). He was an intellectual who tried to lead India to modernity. Ram Mohan played a major role towards abolition of the *sati* or *suttee* system (the custom among some Hindu communities of burning alive the widows in the funeral pyre of their husbands).

Ram Mohan had an elder brother named Jaganmohan. When he died, his widow had to obey the custom of *sati*. When Ram Mohan objected to this, all the people around hum disagreed with him on his stance against *sati*. He tried to persuade his sister-in-law not to observe the ritual, but she followed through with it. Ram Mohan watched helplessly as she screamed and cried as the flames consumed her while she lay next to her dead husband.

Ram Mohan was stricken with remorse afterward. The incident left such an indelible impression on him that it spurred him into action. He vowed to have the practice abolished. He also resolved not to rest until he put an end to this heinous custom. He fought against this practice despite the risks to his life it posed. In the end, he succeeded in making the British colonial government hear his voice. The British listened to him, and abolished it. And so a heartbreaking incident in Ram Mohan's life brought about a great change in his country and in the attitude of some of his fellow men.

When your suffering burns your heart to ashes, a throne is built upon those ashes. Then a radical transformation in your attitude happens that changes your personal outlook on things. Learn from people who have braved the storm like Ram Mohan did. People like Ram Mohan also changed a curse that befell them into a blessing. Everybody on earth is confronted by challenges great and small. Turning curses into blessings is the attitude toward challenges that makes you the master.

There is Wisdom in Your Suffering

Greener on the Other Side

I once went to a clinic hospital in India along with a few other ladies. A man came up to us and introduced himself as a doctor. He said that his dream was to leave India and move to France. Being a doctor is an honorable profession in India. People spend time and invest money to become a doctor. Not every Indian doctor wants to move in a foreign country, but this doctor was not satisfied with his position. He thought that he could be even more successful if he moved to France. He was not aware that many people living in France were going through tough situations.

Some people think that the grass is always greener on the other side of the fence. The mango of your neighbour's garden is always sweeter than yours. Your friend's children are cleverer than your own. You believe that your neighbors are living blissfully, and that only you are in hell. But everybody has problems that may be bigger than yours. Remember: people do not often show their real face. What you see of them in public is not their true self. After having said this, if you do sincerely believe that others are enjoying their life more than you, then learn to share their joy instead of be angry at them. But above all do this: rather than looking at who is better than you on the other side of the fence, take responsibility for your own life instead. Many doors will open for you then.

Growth Requires Responsibility

We do not want to admit that many times we are responsible for our situation. We create our own problems like the elephant, which, after taking a fresh bath, covers itself with dust or throws sand on itself. If you analyze your life honestly, you will find out that you have paved the road to your own misery. Nobody else is responsible for that. You have received a blow for the wrong decision you made, for the attitude you adopted, or for having allowed an unhealthy relationship to be part of your life.

This brings me to another story I have.

The Attitude of the Masters *by Céline Théron*

I was driving in the countryside when my car suddenly stopped in the middle of traffic. There wasn't enough gas in the car. Now I had blocked the road for other drives. The drivers behind me blew their horns, and some even yelled at me. I panicked. Suddenly, a little boy came from I do not know where and said, "There is a garage just on your left. You can push your car until you get there!"

When I turned the car towards the garage while I was pushing it, I discovered the shop was located on a gentle slope. I didn't have to make any effort to push the car, it moved itself.

It is the same with blaming, it requires no effort and it easily takes you downwards. People blame their situation to the point they think doing so helps them with it. It does not. Blaming your situation only gives you a false impression that you are going somewhere with your life. In reality, you are only moving your life downhill, not uphill. To go uphill you have to make an effort. All growth needs effort. And all growth is responsibility. So have a responsible attitude. People accumulate all their mistakes and attribute them to fate. Do not throw your responsibility on fate, God, Karma, society or the economy. Do not blame anybody for your situation. It is the best way to get out of your problems.

Your Black Mark

For the examination of the *baccalauréat* (French High School diploma), I studied many days until late in the evening to be ready for the French literature oral test. On exam day, I crossed the road to reach the high school building. A man carelessly holding a cigarette in his hand collided with me. His cigarette touched my white shirt and left a black mark. I looked at him. He didn't make excuses for his mistake.

The mark was clearly visible. I could not hide it. And the test was about to start in a few minutes.

I finally got to the room where the oral examination was taking place. The examiner called my name. She quickly noticed the black mark on my shirt. She looked at me with a

There is Wisdom in Your Suffering

quizzical expression. I said to myself, "She's probably thinking that I'm not a serious student. All my efforts are lost because of this black mark." Meanwhile, I thought about my eldest sister Claudine, who waited in a prayerful state of mind for my examination result. I did not want to disappoint her. This gave me confidence. I forgot the black mark on my shirt. I kept quiet and waited for the exam question. Once I got it, I completely focused on the test from that point on, and I got a good grade that was above everyone's expectations.

Ask yourself this question: "What black mark is hiding my strength?" We often focus on our black mark even if it is a small one, and forget the wide white part of ourselves which is our strength. To look at your white part and not to your black mark is a great mental attitude.

Our strengths awaken in difficult situations. In a dark night, the stars shine clear because the contrast is there. The kite flies high when the wind blows in its opposite direction. Adversity is your friend that challenges you to realize your full potential.

Face Your Problem Courageously

One of the greatest spiritual leaders, Swami Vivekananda, whose teachings are still spreading all over the world, told an insightful story from his personal life. He related:

> *Once when I was in Varanasi (the holiest city of India), I was passing through a place where there was a large tank of water on one side and a high wall on the other. It was in the grounds where there were many monkeys. The monkeys of Varanasi are huge brutes and are sometimes surly.*
>
> *They now took it into their heads not to allow me to pass through their street, so they howled and shrieked and clutched at my feet as I passed. As they pressed closer, I began to run, but the faster I ran, the faster came the monkeys and they began to bite at me.*
>
> *It seemed impossible to escape, but just then I met a stranger who called out to me, "Face the brutes!" I turned and faced the monkeys, and they fell back and finally fled.*

The Attitude of the Masters *by Céline Théron*

That is a lesson for all life — face the terrible, face it boldly. Like the monkeys, the hardships of life fall back when we cease to flee before them. If we are ever to gain freedom, it must be by conquering nature, never by running away. Cowards never win victories. We have to fight fear and troubles and ignorance if we expect them to flee before us.

We should embrace the moral of this story: We should not run away from our problems. Whenever you escape from something, it follows you. We have to face our problems with a courageous attitude. You can't expect your difficulties to go away by themselves. You have to do something about them. What are you doing to face the problem that blocks your path to success and prevents you from being happy?

You cannot stand still when the house crumbles. You should have the right attitude when life frightens you when you lose work, fail in your business, or separate from someone you are attached to. The world will crush you if you do not have the attitude of a fighter. According to traditional sayings, even gods do not favor the weak. The lion or an elephant is not sacrificed. But a poor sheep is offered in sacrifice. Have you ever seen a sheep brought to the abattoir? It calmly follows the butcher who is going to cut its head with just a small sound: '*maaaaa.*'

Face your problem with the help of someone you trust if needed. If nobody helps you, then face it alone. Many times, you won't get the help you need. Everybody will have deserted you. You will have as a sole friend your own shadow. You have to take your life into your hands. You should have an attitude of a warrior but different from the one in war. Your arsenal is your courage. Your sword is your trust in yourself. Your victory is to prove to yourself that your life has meaning.

Be Flexible Like the Gentle Grass

You do not have fixed strategies or pre-conceived answers to everything you will face. In some situations you have to face your problems. Sometimes, it is wiser to surrender. Are you

There is Wisdom in Your Suffering

a fighter and think that it is cowardice to surrender? It is not negative and cowardly to surrender. It just means that you are mature and courageous enough to let yourself be taken by the flow of life without fighting. The masters do not hesitate to bend like the gentle grass when it is necessary.

Be as flexible as the gentle grass to win through the hardships of life. You have to understand that there are things you cannot change even though you fight. Instead of fighting, have an attitude of acceptance. Take for example this aspect of nature: A great storm comes, and big trees fall. The big trees resist, fighting to show their strength. They do not want to surrender. On the contrary, the gentle grass bends with grace to the storm which it has no power over. When the storm is gone, the small plants and grass are very clean and fresh.

Blaise Pascal said, "Man is but a reed, the most feeble thing in nature, but he is a thinking reed." Likewise, man is frail like a flower outside. However, he's a strong spiritual being. He can win if he's flexible enough to surrender. People sometimes think that it is a force to be hard so they are rigid and refuse to surrender. They want to be as hard as the rock. The rock is hard but dead. The flower is not as strong as the rock. It is frail but alive. If the flower clashes against the rock, it will be defeated. But the flower can also win. The flower wins with its own ways that is not fighting but surrendering. The reed is frail but strong because it is flexible. A flexible attitude is one the keys of the masters to overcoming obstacles.

CHAPTER SEVEN

Persist Until You Succeed

Persist Until You Succeed

On a sunny day, a young boy called Bhim and his brother Anand had to travel to Goregaon to meet their father who was working as a cashier. They decided to hire a bullock-cart but the cart-men did not want to carry the boys. Finally, Bhim and Anand promised to pay double the usual cost of the journey. One of the cart men agreed to take them to their father but on the condition they drove the cart themselves. The cart man followed on foot beside the cart.

Bhim never forgot this incident.

At school, Bhim had to sit on the floor in one corner in the classroom, away from other pupils. His sister had to cut his hair at home because the village barbers who cut even the hair of a buffalo would not touch Bhim's hair. Once, the young Bhim felt unbearable thirst. There was a wellspring near him. He drank water from the well. Someone found him and cried, "Go away! Go away!" People gathered and beat the boy pitilessly.

People humiliated him again and again. These bitter

The Attitude of the Masters *by Céline Théron*

experiences were etched onto the boy's sensitive mind. Bhim did not know why he should be treated differently.

What was wrong with Bhim?

Bhim was born in the Mahar caste, which was considered as the lowest of the low. Bhim was treated as *untouchable* by the upper class. However, this young boy became a barrister. His name is Bhimrao Ambedkar. Later, he became Law Minister in independent India. Dr. Ambedkar was a great Indian leader who fought for the rights and equality of people called *untouchable*. He prepared the Constitution in such a way so to establish social and economic equality in the Indian society.

Perseverance was one of his most important qualities that raised him from low caste to a high position in society. The attitude of perseverance is the secret key of all masters to get victories. No matter who you are and where you come from, with perseverance, every person can make their dream a reality. I've heard people say that they gave up because they did everything in their power, yet did not succeed. Making a genuine effort means to not stop until you attain success.

Ask yourself this: What can you improve inside yourself to the point where you are ready to move to the next level? You do not need to take a leap, but proceed step by step. As Francis of Assisi says, "Start by doing what's necessary; then do what's possible; and suddenly you are doing the impossible." If the path is right, you are certain to be successful.

Know the Path You Walk On

In a one-way Indian traffic road lit only by car lights, a drunken man stumbled in front of an oncoming lorry. The lorry driver desperately turned the steering wheel and barely avoided an accident. The driver then stopped the lorry beside the drunken man. The driver had been so startled by the drunken man's attitude that his shirt was soaked with sweat. He opened the door and said to the drunken man, "Hey, look where you are going! Do you want to go to heaven?"

Persist Until You Succeed

You cannot go on the path of life unconsciously like the drunken man. If you do not have a clear vision of where you are going, why you are going, and what you are looking for, you might end up on the wrong direction and be left dead on the side of the road. Know the path you are walking on. If you are walking on the right path, the light of faith will help you to overcome the obstacles that might block your way.

Your Faith Is Your Inner Lighthouse

Have faith and hope in dark moments. Faith is your inner lighthouse that guides you through the dark.

In my village, nighttime was always very dark. There were no streetlights. The pathway was dangerous. We had to stumble on stones, walk on thorns, and we could cross a wandering dog. My home was surrounded by many huts that were lit only by dim lanterns. When we were lost on the road, the light from the lantern hanging on the walls of the huts lighted up the street. This slight light coming from each house illuminated the way home for us.

When you walk alone surrounded by the darkness of life, you have to keep fire of your faith burning inside you because faith has the power to light up the path of man just like those lanterns lit the way home for my sister and me on those dark nights.

There is a beautiful story from Mohammed's life that shows the power of faith. Mohammed is followed by his enemies. He and his friend try to escape in the dead of night. They hide in a cave. They can hear the sounds of the horses' hooves. The enemy is coming closer and closer. There seems to be no escape. The friend is perspiring, afraid that they would soon be discovered but Mohammed remains perfectly calm. The friend asks, "Are you not afraid? We are only two." Mohammed replies, "We are not two but three with God." In this extremely critical situation, where there is a question of life and death, Mohammed has not despaired.

Now there is noise at the mouth of the cave. They hear a

The Attitude of the Masters *by Céline Théron*

voice outside saying, "Nobody can be hidden in here. The entrance is covered with spider's webs, nests and branches." This misleads the enemy, and they decide to search for Mohammed and his friend elsewhere.

By keeping the fires of his faith blazing bright inside him even when his enemies were outside the cave entrance, God blessed Mohammed with a miracle.

When an abyss is in front of you and a precipice is behind, would you still have an unwavering faith that you will come out of the situation alive? The masters with their trustful attitude achieved even the impossible. Gandhi led his people into freedom without taking weapons against the British Empire because he had a profound faith in God, in his mission, and in *Ahimsa*, which called for non-violence.

The miracle happens when you have faith in the Infinite. However, you should never forget that the Universe is waiting to help you until you make the first step: have faith in yourself.

Today, we have much more than past generations. However, many of us are living in anxiety. People have many things, but one thing has left their heart. It is trust. They have doubt about their future. They do not even trust the husband or wife with whom they live. They have doubt about everything.

The Universe trusts you. Even if you want to end your life and throw yourself in the river, nature gives you three chances. You come out of the water three times before disappearing beneath the surface. Although the whole universe trusts you and you do not have faith in yourself, you cannot move an inch in life. Let a man go down as low as possible; there must come a time when out of sheer desperation he will take an upward curve and will learn to have faith in himself. Do you have to go down to prove to yourself that you will come up? Why not trust in yourself now?

One day, a blind lady was lost in the street. I went close to her and seized her arm to help her cross the road. She got angry. She strongly shook my hand and said, "I don't need any help. I can manage myself." I apologized and took leave

Persist Until You Succeed

from her. I misunderstood the lady. She was not a blind woman standing on the corner, waiting for someone to lead her across the road. She was confident that she could cross the road alone. I appreciated her confident attitude.

We all sometimes need help, but even if there is a crew on the ship to help you navigate, you are the captain of the ship. Others can give you guidance, but you have to walk on the road with confidence like a master. If you are thirsty, you have to drink. No one can do it for you. Having faith in yourself is the foundation on which you can build your life.

When others doubt you, have faith in yourself. In your path, you are bound to meet many fortune tellers making cynical predictions for your life. Do not listen to them. Make their predictions false instead of helping make them come true by believing such lies.

A French teacher in my elementary school once told me, "Céline, if you go until middle school I will resign my job!" This teacher's words did not prevent me from becoming a Law graduate. I did whatever it took to succeed in my study.

One day, I had a difficult mathematics exercise for homework. I asked a lady in the street, "Madame, can you please help me with this exercise?" She was surprised that a young child could ask someone in the street to help to do her homework. She answered, "Of course, with pleasure."

Your success is like a kite. Your talent is the wind that helps it fly high. And the thread you hold is your faith in yourself. If the thread breaks, then your success will fall down by itself no matter how talented you are.

Have you ever seen a flower garland? You can see the flowers, but you cannot see the thread. But it is the hidden thread inside the garland that holds the whole garland together. Similarly, the masters have a secret thread within their hearts that is their faith in them. Therefore, the masters accomplish great missions.

It does not mean that if you have a trustful attitude you will never fail. Your faith helps you to overcome the obstacles, but you will inevitably stumble now and then while on your way to success.

Be Willing To Fall Down

The life of man is like the waves of the ocean. The waves can rise high and then fall again. The process to achieve success is the same because you will find both the highs of success and the lows of failure. But the stones that make you stumble and fall down are actually *stepping stones*, not obstacles. So your attitude should be of someone who is not afraid to fall down.

Sometimes when you resist falling, you can hurt yourself. When a bullock cart's wheel is trapped in a hole and there is an accident, a drunken man riding in the cart is barely hurt, whereas other passengers can have serious injuries. The drunken man did not resist because he fell out of the cart like a pile of cotton. His mind is in security. He does not have fear.

When we were kids, even when we fell down in the midst of people we did not feel uncomfortable. We went up to them to show where we were hurt and expected consolation and aid from them. Adults acknowledged our pain. They said kind words and caressed us. Then, we felt no more pain. Life was so simple. Why is it complicated now? Everything is different when we grow up. When an adult falls down, she is embarrassed. She looks around her to see if someone has noticed. If there is any witness she feels ashamed. Why is it so hard to accept a simple body movement? The kids fall down many times a day. They do not hurt themselves too much because they do not resist it.

You have to put aside your pride and be without shame. "Our greatest glory is not in never falling, but in rising every time we fall." This is the wise teaching of Confucius. The master, Jesus Christ, fell down three times while on his way to Golgotha, but he kept getting up again and again. After his falling, his rising was great. Today, millions of people after more than two thousand years still remember his glory and victory. Falling does not mean failing. The masters fall down but they know they must get up again and again. If you fall down on the ground, use the ground itself for support to stand up. Your attitude can change any embarrassing situation into a favorable one.

Transform the Venom into Medicine
We can choose our attitude whatever our circumstances are. We do not have the power to change the outside circumstances that surround us. But we can act on our attitude. It is the only thing that we have power over. Adopt the attitude of the master whatever the circumstances are.

It is reported that when William the Conqueror was leaping from his boat to the shore, he stumbled and fell. His companions were greatly troubled at his mishap, which seemed to them an ill omen. He who has so great a thing to accomplish in England should not, they thought, stumble and fall as soon as he touched its shore. But William lifted his hands, which were full of earth, and cried in a loud voice, "See! As soon as I put my feet on this land I have taken possession of this land of England!"

When you adopt the attitude of the masters you can change a bad omen into a good one. Epictetus says, "A black cat augurs happiness if you want it to." It is a question of attitude. Your attitude can change the venom into medicine, a problem into a solution.

In your journey to attaining success, you can fall asleep because the way to it can be long. The attitude of perseverance is fruitful if you remain alert along the way. Otherwise, you can miss many opportunities. Then, it will be difficult for you to reach the harbor.

Be Alert When Opportunity Knocks On Your Door
Most of time, people live by habits. They drive to the office and return home almost unconsciously. They are going through life as if they are sleeping. But how long can these

The Attitude of the Masters *by Céline Théron*

people remain asleep?

Once while my father was coming home, something bit him above his ankle. As there were no streetlights, he could not see, but he knew that it was a snake bite. He caught sight of the head of a snake in the darkness. He always had a pocket knife with him for such emergencies. He took his knife out and cut the snake in two.

We only wake up in life-threatening situations like those my father faced with the snake. Why? Because our minds become fully alert only when we are in danger, not out of it. The rest of time we live unconsciously.

The masters remain alert. Life requires us to be alert at all times. If not, you will pass by many opportunities without seeing them, and you will only feel deep remorse when you realize what that opportunity was long after you passed it.

Opportunity visits you when you do not expect it, so always be prepared to seize it. Opportunity knocks at your door at night, asking for shelter like a man who escaped from a heavy rain and looking for a refuge. If you are asleep and do not heed the knock, it will go and knock at the door of someone who is not asleep. Nurture an alert mind. He who tries to seize an opportunity after it has passed by is like one who sees it approach but will not go to meet it. Be alert to go and meet it when the opportunity approaches you.

I remember an incident back when I was a little girl. The sun well up in the sky when I awoke that day to the sounds of our village. The women talked shrilly at the public fountain on the street, and the milk man was delivering milk from house to house.

In our garden, there were huge coconuts trees that gave shadow even in hot seasons. There were the henhouse and the rabbit hutches. My dad was breeding chickens, rabbits and turkeys. He had cultivated all kind of vegetables and even some fruits. In the air floated the odor of bananas. Birds were chattering and two crows passed over my head and sat on the branch of a tree.

Persist Until You Succeed

Near the garden was the kitchen. Mama served my breakfast in the garden. She had prepared me *idli* (a savory salted cake) with coconut chutney. We did not always use plates. She served me the food on a banana leaf and cut a tender coconut fruit for the water. She left me alone for a few minutes. The crow was looking at me with its sharp eyes while I got ready to eat the *idli*. It suddenly swooped down and snatched the *idli* from my hand, scratching my face with one of its talons in the process.

I lost my food in the distance between my hand and my mouth. That's what happens when you are not alert in life. The opportunity can slip from your hands in the twinkling of an eye, and then you will not have time to catch it back. What is in your hand can be grasped by somebody else like the crow did and leave a scratch in your mind. The opportunity will come to you but it will not remain forever. If you do not keep a little alert it will be gone soon. To keep walking on the way to success, you need also to have a watchful and cheerful attitude.

Have a Cheerful Attitude

You have to be enthusiastic to achieve your goals. The word enthusiasm has a divine origin. The source of the word is in the Greek language. It means *having the god within* in Greek. When you do something with deep enthusiasm, God is within you. Bring enthusiasm to what you are doing. If you are dull in what you are doing, you can't stay on track for a long time.

Do everything with a cheerful attitude. Enthusiasm gives you a positive energy to move ahead. Kids are enthusiastic, no matter if something is ordinary or not, for everything is always extraordinary to them. Youths have so much energy because they have a cheerful attitude. I saw a boy once say to his mother, "This summer, I devoured one book a day!" His mother corrected him, "We do not devour a book. We read it." She did not understand the enthusiasm and the energy her son possessed. Adults try to transform children so that they become as dull and flat as them. Youth are never satisfied because they expect more from life. They believe that existence has something more to give to them.

When we were kids we had dreams and believed even in the impossible. I remember keeping a peacock feather in my school notebook. It is said that it has a positive effect on a kid's performance in their studies. People told me that it gives birth to more peacock feathers. In India, many children believe in that story. I fed the feather with grains of rice. I used to check it regularly to see if it reproduced. Even when it did not happen after many years had passed, my hope and belief that it would happen one day remained unshaken. Nobody could take away my enthusiasm in taking care of the feather.

When we grow up we lose such enthusiasm. Some people even develop an attitude of failure. Therefore, they do not believe in other's dreams. They will justify their attitude by their experiences. But the question is not about the number of experiences but the quality of the experience. The experience of a single thing done with enthusiasm has a divine quality.

However motivated and enthusiastic you might be, if the journey is too long, you might get tired. Your journey of hundred miles becomes easier if you make it just two miles.

Just Two Miles

A man and his servant went on a journey on foot. They were dressed in traditional attire, white cotton *dhoti* or *vesthi* (a long, loose loincloth) along with a shirt and a *thundu* (or *angavastara*, long piece of cloth draped around the shoulders.) They had for meals tamarind rice (a delicious tangy-spicy dish) which is known for its great travel food.

Suddenly a few bandits living in the forest attacked them. They used to steal the possessions of people passing by. The men said, "Please do not do any harm to us. We do not have any valuables." The bandits were frustrated. Without a qualm, they took the two traveler's food parcels and a few rupees and

Persist Until You Succeed

then the bandits left.

After walking miles, the man and his servant were tired. They had nothing to eat. A mother and her young son carrying wood passed throughout the forest. The servant asked them, "How far is the town from here?" The son said, "The town is quite far, at least fifteen miles." Fifteen miles? Hearing this, the man and the servant sat on a rock exhausted. The mother intervened, "Oh, no! It is not as far. It is just two miles." She looked at her son and whispered, "Look how tired they are. Make it two miles." When the man and the servant heard, "Just two miles," they were eager to continue their journey.

Just two miles is the secret of life. My eldest sister Claudine, who took great care of me when I was very young, knew that secret instinctively. When I could not walk, I asked my sister to carry me. The way was just too long for a little girl like me. My sister said, "Honey, walk a little. We have just arrived." Every time I asked her to carry me, she said, "We will arrive soon." Finally, I walked the whole distance. She could not tell me the whole truth because I would not be able to bear it and I would stop walking.

The attitude of the man who goes the extra mile is this: He says to himself, "Just two miles." To achieve what you want in life can take time. You have to walk a long distance. Say to yourself, "Just two miles!" or "I will soon arrive." If you move from two miles to another two miles, it will make your long journey easier. As Lao Tzu says, "A journey of a thousand miles begins with a single step. By taking one step after another you complete your journey however far it is."

Build It Again

During your journey, things will not always go as you want. You can lose the harvest of your life in a short time. In my countryside school in France, we little girls and boys played marbles together. In this game, I won hundreds of marbles of different sizes and colors. I gathered them in a cotton bag

The Attitude of the Masters *by Céline Théron*

that I kept in my room under my bed. It was like my own private treasure. At home, sometimes, we had arguments between children about marbles. My dad had a strict notion of discipline. One time he threw my bag of marbles through the window. And so something I had invested much time in accumulating was lost in a minute.

It takes time to build something. A second is enough to destroy what you have built. You can lose everything in a few minutes.

I remember when I was a kid in my village in India. I'd seen villagers working hard in their fields. When harvest time came, sometimes jealous neighbours crushed the grown crops or lit the fields on fire at night. The farmers who suffered such depredations lost in a few minutes all their crops. And if they escaped from people's jealous attitudes, they were caught by natural disasters. It seemed like every year a terrible storm would destroy the entire village as if it were a ruthless tyrant. What the villagers had labored to build was devastated in a heartbeat.

However, they were resilient people. They said, "We will rebuild this village again!" What a persevering attitude!

People who are result-oriented have a practical attitude. They take every step to achieve their goals and get results. But the same people are shuttered when they have to face loss because it has a negative impact on their mind.

What do you do when the harvest of your hard work is destroyed in a few minutes? Never give up. Rebuild it again. Rebuilding is more difficult than building. Masters have the attitude of building anew from the ruins.

It is reported that Isaac Newton had kept on his table papers gathering the results of his many years of research. One day, his dog pushed a lighted candle onto the table which fell on the papers. Isaac Newton was pained to see his long time work turned into ashes, but he persevered. He repeated the experiment. We should have the same attitude as Newton to rebuild what was destroyed.

Persist Until You Succeed

I remember observing little birds sheltered in the trees of my garden. They'd go and take twig after another twig and build alone their nests and seek protection on the bough of a tree. But the pitiless storm would come and ruin the nests of these little birds. They would find themselves as ruined as the villagers, but they'd rebuild their nests and live peacefully again. If the little birds can build again, can't human beings do it? One who does not give up and keeps persevering in the face of adversity will find unexpected help.

Unexpected Help Will Come

The traffic in town was blocked. People were running here and there. Angry yelling arose from the crowd. It was a violent strike in the streets. My mother and I were in a rickshaw stopped on this street. I saw a group of men blindly going through the crowd and hitting people without distinction with a stick.

One of them ran toward us as a wild beast with a thick wood stick on his hand. I was a kid at that time but I still vividly remember him. He raised his stick to hit us when his hand stopped a few inches from my head. I was terrified and screamed. He said to Mama, "Move on quickly from here." He let us go without any harm. We did not know what happened. What stopped his hand? God had stopped his hand and protected our lives.

We cannot see the wind but the dancing leaves show the invisible power behind them. In the same, an invisible force is here to help you. When you do your best like a master in life, an unexpected help will come. There is a saying, "Six steps are human effort, and the seventh is divine grace!" You can call it luck, mystery or God. The name does not matter, but be sure that when you persevere, a higher power will help you accomplish your destiny. Your attitude of perseverance will bring you where you aim to be.

CHAPTER EIGHT
The Laws of Nature

The Laws of Nature

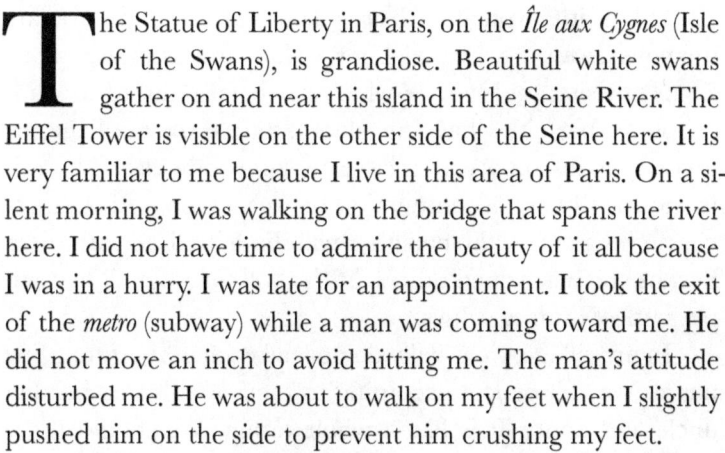

The Statue of Liberty in Paris, on the *Île aux Cygnes* (Isle of the Swans), is grandiose. Beautiful white swans gather on and near this island in the Seine River. The Eiffel Tower is visible on the other side of the Seine here. It is very familiar to me because I live in this area of Paris. On a silent morning, I was walking on the bridge that spans the river here. I did not have time to admire the beauty of it all because I was in a hurry. I was late for an appointment. I took the exit of the *metro* (subway) while a man was coming toward me. He did not move an inch to avoid hitting me. The man's attitude disturbed me. He was about to walk on my feet when I slightly pushed him on the side to prevent him crushing my feet.

I looked behind me after few steps. The man was standing still. I asked myself, "Why did he stop?" I walked back up to him and looked at his face. He was thoughtful. He seemed to be confused. I realized that the man could not see. In my hurry and anxiety, I had become blind as well.

I approached him and touched his shoulder. He felt that it was me.

I said, "Forgive me, sir."

The Attitude of the Masters *by Céline Théron*

He replied, "No, problem." He had a great attitude.

I told him, "I'd like to help you to go upstairs."

He was happy that I accompanied him. I was not in a hurry anymore. Suddenly, I had plenty of time to spare.

In the subway, in a few minutes you are bound to run with the crowd even without any reason. In big cities, everybody is in such a hurry. You will feel that something is wrong with you by moving slowly. "Hurry up!" seems to be the watchword. The modern life is speed, speed, and speed. Many of us have a running attitude. Where are you running so fast? The life of the man is not always a smooth road. Better to slow down when on a steep path. All sensible people use their brakes in life. Most of us have more time than we think. The masters who revealed great truths led the busiest of lives, but they could find time to realize them and to teach them to humanity. This is what Buddha always did.

In big cities, you are in a crowd but still a stranger. You are unknown even to your neighbors. Many are as utterly alone as an unvisited old temple which has been reduced to ruins. People in big cities have an aloof attitude. In a village, everybody is in some way related to somebody else. There is friendship. There is communion between people. If a family has nothing to eat, the neighbor will share his food with them. Because he has helped others, others will help him. They simply respect human values.

In my village, we usually do not call each other by our first name. We call people according to their ages, sister, brother, uncle and aunty. It is like a whole family. We should move back to our villages. We are all living in a village. Your home is a village. Your workplace is a village. Your social club is a village. Your sport center is a village. Your school is a village. Your group of friends is a village. You have to come close to the laws of the nature like the villagers.

Follow the Rhythm of Life

Everything lives on earth according to the Laws of Nature,

The Laws of Nature

and out of those laws emerges harmony in life; but man set a limited and earthly law of his own. The laws of nature are rhythm and not speed. The rhythm is needed to live fully your life. Stop a moment, and then you will realize that you should not hurry but instead follow the eternal laws of nature that is rhythm.

The day turns into night. It is a rhythm. In the day, you are awake, in the night you are asleep. It is a rhythm. The animals follow the laws of nature. The lion eats only when it is hungry. After the hunt, when the lion has eaten its prey, it is lying on the ground, licking its lips. Likewise, you can't go on eating. You eat and during the sleeping hours, you fast. It is a rhythm.

You have lost the rhythm. You have lost your balance. Life is a rhythm between rest and action. Have an active attitude, but do not forget that inaction is needed as much as action. Action done totally brings relaxation. When your mind and body are resting, it brings more energy and action.

The rhythm between words and silence is also needed. We live in the world of words. There is no room for silence. The attitude of the communicator is not only talking and talking. The pause, the silence in your communication is powerful. Your attitude is much more important than your words. You do not always need to talk to prove that you know something. Lao-Tzu says, "Those who know do not speak. Those who speak do not know." Sometimes, take the wise attitude to be an active listener. Move from the world of words to the world of silence.

The Song of the Silence

We often hear many voices of the world that appeal to us. Sometimes, we need to have the attitude of silence to find out which call to answer. Gandhi says, "In the attitude of silence the soul finds the path in a clearer light, and what is elusive and deceptive resolves itself into crystal clearness." The attitude of silence is an expression of our profound being.

The Attitude of the Masters *by Céline Théron*

The western culture is not familiar with the attitude of silence. Now the general attitude is to feel that we do not really understand what we cannot represent, or what we cannot communicate. The language of words has its utility but also its limits. In the midst of the crowd, man is lonely because communication has failed. We need to learn the language of silence. Silence is not a communication but a communion.

Great values lose their sacred quality when you try to express them by words. How to express in the language the innermost feeling in the heart of man? In a moment of overwhelming love, you find that there is nothing to be said in words. The word love is needed only when love is missing. When you become love, you have an attitude of silence. In the same vein, a true feeling of gratitude can hardly be communicated by the language of words.

The first time I was in London, I ignored the fact that the heater was precious in the city of London. The owner of the apartment did not want to heat the flat because it would cost her money. It was winter, and it was so cold in the flat that I became sick. There was a kind girl called Stella who lived in the same building as me. She told me, "I can help you to find a new flat." I was a little lost in this new city. So she took time to look at the advertisements. Stella called the owner to make an appointment for visiting the flat. She accompanied me. I did not like the flat after the visit.

Stella comforted me saying, "Don't worry darling. We will find a good one." Her help and kindness profoundly touched me. I looked at her silently. In our way home, I noted a change in her expression. I asked her, "Is something wrong?" Stella answered sincerely, "I am surprised that you did not say thank you to me. In my country, we say thank you when someone helps."

I understood the lady. She was not accustomed with the attitude of silence. She expected me to say, "Thank you!" in words. But I was so grateful to her, my whole being expressed my gratitude to her silently but deeply.

The Laws of Nature

We live on words. We have turned everything into formalities. Since we do not understand the attitude of silence, we follow the ritual of words. In my culture, we do not say, "Thank you!" to our parents. We touch their feet; by this gesture, we express our thankfulness.

When an emotion is too strong, it is extremely hard to put it into words. When you are in deep sorrow or in great happiness, tears flow. It is the language of silence. The attitude of mind is word. The emotions come from the depth of the heart. The attitude of the heart is silence.

Listen to the song of silence. Let your sensibility be touched by the silence around you. The grandiose sun that gives light to the entire world is silent. A flower blossoms in silence. The stars move in silence. Listen to the silence of the night. Embrace the beauty of the silence. It brings peace to the turmoil of our lives. The attitude of silence helps you to go inwards and live a meditative life.

The Meditative Attitude

Being meditative requires a change in your attitude. Your great challenge here is just to sit for a few minutes and not do anything. It is difficult for the jittery minds and agitated bodies to just remain sitting. It seems unnatural, sitting just to sit. There is nothing unnatural to remain sitting calmly. If you observe the kingdom of animals, the king of the forest, the lion, can remain sitting without hunting. In our house, the dog is sitting for a long time. In my village, peasants were sitting outside the house, gossiping without qualms of conscience that they were wasting their time. It was the most valuable time they spent with their families and neighbours. Despite their hard toil until late in the evening, they had enough time to rest, to relax and even to be lazy. Do not always carry a result-oriented mind, but become as childlike as village people gossiping and playing, not interested in the end result.

The *Dhyana* (meditation) is a great way to curb your restless mind. This spiritual exercise is where you sit with your legs

The Attitude of the Masters *by Céline Théron*

crossed and your feet resting. You must remain sitting so there is nothing else to be done. For people in a hurry, sitting and meditating do not have any appeal. It is a hard discipline for them. When you are capable of sitting and experiencing the world with the mind completely at rest, you live fully.

People feel that sitting still for hours on end is a great waste of precious time. They think that they ought to be doing something more important to grow. It is hard to see how one can transform the world for the better and make a difference by keeping still.

The Zen poem says: "Sitting quietly, doing nothing, spring comes, and the grass grows by itself." Buddha was sitting quietly under a tree, meditating, but he attained the Enlightenment. He brought the best possible contributions to a world in the quest for true meaning. With a meditative attitude, you touch your soul. Then, you are yourself.

Accept Your Uniqueness

The masters accept their uniqueness. They are not afraid to be themselves. We flee nothing as much as ourselves. You need courage to be as you are in any situation. Anyone who has respect for himself will have a genuine attitude. You do not need to imitate anybody. Nature is not an imitation. The cactus does not imitate the rose flower. You are part of nature. Let your attitude be authentic. Dare to be different and original. Why should we be afraid of it?

In my village, I was in contact with different tribal people. Early each morning, a mysterious man used to pass by my house. He was the soothsayer. His face was fearful. He had on strange, scary-looking make-up. He wore the beaded necklace, a powerful red *tilakam* on his forehead, a colorful dress and a turban. His distinctive attire not only surprised but also scared many people who never met him at that time. Women, who had to go to the public fountain for water, woke up at three o'clock in the morning to fill up their pots before he came. He wandered the streets, stopping at each doorstep to spell out

The Laws of Nature

good and bad predictions. He recited the sooth in a poetic manner, all the while rattling the Damarutham he carried.

I always woke up whenever I heard the ear-piercing sound from his small rattle Damarutham. I was scared whenever I saw him. Mama warned me many times that I should never approach him because he kidnapped children. Many strange stories like this were told about the soothsayers. It was said that these people knew magic, that they performed rituals in a graveyard, or that they have a magic black cream to seduce people with. Today, I know that all these stories are simply rumors.

People from another tribe also passed through my village. They were wearing a tin can over their hips, and generally had a very unclean look. They were like primitive people living off of hunting. They hunted foxes and birds. They ate all kinds of animals, rats, turkeys, and hares. They mostly survived thanks to the selling of animals' teeth, beaded necklaces or handmade ladies small cloth wallets. From this tribe, an old woman named Digli Bai went throughout our village. She often visited Mama. In our tradition, we do not call elderly people by their names. So I called her grandma. She kindly tied a fox's teeth necklace around my neck. The old lady seemed to come from a strange far land. She told us interesting stories about life in her tribe.

These people are excluded from the rest of the population because of ethnic reasons. The society that marginalizes these tribal people can learn a lot from them. They have great human values. There is no room for the word widow in their tribe. If a woman has lost her husband, she can marry another man. The baby girls are welcomed, and women are treated as equally as men.

They are interesting people, just different. Unfortunately, they are put aside because of their difference. Difference is the essence of life. It is variety that makes this earth beautiful. The people of these tribes are good, simple, beautiful and innocent. They show themselves as they are, not as others wish to see them. They have an authentic attitude. Modernity did not have much impact on them. They still remain close to their ancestors and nature. They are original.

Your difference is your uniqueness. Accept your uniqueness. It is a gift. Nobody like you was already born or will be born. We are afraid to be original. We are often preoccupied by other people's opinions and try to fit our attitude to their criterion.

Be yourself. You are here to fulfill your own destiny, which is individual. Do not impose someone else's personality upon you. Taking inspiration from a role model does not mean that you are born to be merely the shade or copy of them. You grow to be nobody else but yourself. You are beautiful and strong in your own way. Learn from successful people. Get education, motivation and inspiration from them. However, it is better to be the best you rather than be a copy of your role model.

Our modern world incites people to imitate others. It encourages people to live like they are youths. Many people are uncomfortable when getting old. They are looking for a magic potion to keep them young forever. Old age has its own beauties, just as youth has its own beauties. We make houses or hospitals for old people where they are left alone as if they are worthless. Elderly people have learned many secrets of life. They can be great teachers. We can learn wisdom from their life experiences.

In my countryside, people were at ease with being old. They were proud to have lived their lives. They had the respect of others. We loved to hear their stories. The Indian tradition encourages them to take up a spiritual journey by abandoning conventional life after the duties of family and citizenship have been fulfilled by a certain age so they can trade household life for another, more significant purpose.

Our consumer society has taken away the originality of people by encouraging them to imitate their idols. It makes people dream to live as somebody else. People do the same

The Laws of Nature

thing as others do. Life has no more thrills. In the city, people have locked the door to real excitements.

Welcome Your Visitors with Excitement
The doors of the houses in my village were not bolted. Their gates were always open. People did not fear that someone would steal their possessions. Openness was their custom. The most beautiful part of this custom was the surprise visit of a guest. Our tradition says that we should welcome a person who comes to our house even though he is our worst enemy. The welcoming attitude of the villagers brought joy and thrill in life.

One day, some relatives of Mama suddenly came home. Mama was so happy to see them, she quickly sent the maid to the market to buy what she needed to cook for lunch. Mama quickly made lunch as soon as the maid had returned. Afterward, mama and her guests sat around discussing things for a long time before her relatives departed.

The guest simply comes and knocks at the door. There is a great joy to suddenly see a friend at your doorstep. It is a surprise. But in our modern life, everything is predicted. Nobody can just suddenly knock at your door even though you are available. They have to take an appointment before coming. Everything has to be arranged in advance. Then, life becomes boring.

Man in the city made strict rules for himself. He built a narrow and painful prison in which he locked his happiness. He dug out a deep grave in which he buried his heart and affections. He is eager to live in a grave in the name of "safety" and "security." But there is no more wonder left in your life when you close the door to keep the unknown outside.

The surprise guest was one of the beauties in the villagers' life. Open the gate and celebrate life with others.

Celebrate the Life You Have
Celebrate life. Our modern world does not know the joy of

The Attitude of the Masters *by Céline Théron*

real celebration. People are satisfied with a substitute such as entertainment, watching television, or few days off for the holidays. But life is meant to be lived fully. Do not be satisfied with a substitute for celebration. Celebration is much more than entertainment or diversion.

Life is celebration. Your life becomes celebration when you return to your source, which is nature. Stress and tension dissipate when you are close to nature. You experience a peaceful enjoyment while in touch with Mother Nature. But in our city life, we have lost sensibility for nature.

What makes the life of a peasant a joy to them is that they are living in harmony with nature. They do not have an alarm clock. The song of the rooster, "cock-a-doodle-doo" awakens them. You are told the value of gold but not the value of the moon, but they peasants do when they savor sleeping under the moonlight.

The rainy day does not give them a dull mood. Their kids always find joy in dancing and walking barefoot without an umbrella in the rain. A cheerful panic usually broke out in my village whenever such a shower started. During bigger storms, we all turned towards the door whenever the lightning began to flash across the sky. Such storms frightened us so much that for protection from the thunderstorm we cried, "Arjuna! Arjuna!" Arjuna was one of the most striking characters in the *Mahabharata* (a Hindu epic). After the storm, the silence was beautiful. The rainwater that flowed down the street formed a little river. I loved to sit on the veranda to watch it flow on the step of my house. I made boats with paper to sail on it and enjoyed picking up things that floated down the river that the storm had left behind it.

We have lost the attitude of wonder. We have to become kids again to recapture the wonder of life. The child is astonished at the beauty of the earth. He sees everything for the first time. Everything seems miraculous to him. He runs joyfully after the butterflies. He is amazed to see the stones we walk on. He collects them as diamonds. In the true man, there is a child hidden inside. He wants to play. Let him play. Sometimes, you should simply allow yourself to be like a child.

Life is *leela* (play.) The life is play for the masters. For the master Krishna life is *leela*. Even in fight, he was playful. You do not need to prove you are an expert all day long, so take some time to play with kids. They can help you to live as fully as they do. For example, the people in my village amused themselves idly with the same activities as kids once their daily toil was over.

We did not always go to movies. Sometimes, a wandering man would come with a big box. Through a small window in it, we saw a film that played as the man turned a handle on the box. Other times, street dancers would pass through the village. We gathered on the streets and enjoyed their dance. People threw money on a mat that the dancers had put out.

The villagers celebrated life in a simple way. Celebration does not have to be expensive. Our nights of celebration did not take place in restaurants or in night clubs, but simply on the streets. We did not pay for a concert or theatre ticket to watch others playing. We were not spectators. We had an active attitude of participation, that we were actors. There is great joy in being totally involved in celebration, such as the time my village staged the play *Karna*. Karna was the great tragic hero of *Mahabharata*, well known for his generosity. I remember in particular how we played the crucial scene where Karna met for the first time his mother Kunti, who had placed Karna in a basket when he had been born and set him afloat in a river. Even children had small roles in the play. It was a far cry from the passive "entertainment" people have to "celebrate" things with today.

The attitude of celebration enlivens the heart of man. Have the attitude of the masters. Transform small things into celebration. Each moment is an opportunity to celebrate life. Whatever you are doing, do it playfully and cheerfully. And wherever you are, be in a celebratory mood. Do not put any

The Attitude of the Masters *by Céline Théron*

condition to celebrate life. Celebration is your attitude, unconditional as to what life brings. Your attitude as a master can transform your life into one of pure celebration.

CHAPTER NINE

Journey Into Your Inner World

Journey Into Your Inner World

The Futuroscope is among the largest theme parks at Poitiers, France. Among many wonderful attractions, there was an adventure called *Les yeux grand fermes*. It was a journey into the dark. We explored different worlds as a blind man guided us along a new route cloaked in darkness. We experienced an extraordinary adventure that took us from the Louisiana bayou to vibrant New York City, and up to the highest Himalayan peak. You smell, listen, touch and 'see' the world in a new way. After the journey, while walking to the exit, we read the following quote: "The essential is invisible to the eyes." – Saint Antoine d'Exupery. That was the lesson of this journey through darkness.

The Essential is Invisible to the Eyes

Many times, we consider what we see is important, but the essential is invisible to the eyes. What we often search for are visible things such as money, power, and prestige. The spiritual values are invisible but essential. It does not mean that we have to ignore what is tangible. The visible and invisible are like the body and soul of man.

The Attitude of the Masters *by Céline Théron*

Do not have an extreme attitude. Any extreme is not good for a human. When there is too much light you are dazzled. When it is too dark, you can't see. The masters know to follow the middle path. The middle *pada* (path) was the great truth that Siddhartha found. For six years, Siddhartha was meditating in the forest. For drink, he had rainwater. For food, he had a grain of rice. One day, Siddhartha heard an old musician on a passing boat impart this bit of wisdom to his pupil: "When the string is too tight, it will snap. If the string is very loose, the music cannot arise." Siddhartha realized that these simple words convey a great truth. He abandoned the extreme asceticism he was following and chose the middle way that he would teach to the world. Life in the middle way lies between two opposite extremes. Man is between pleasure and blissfulness, the finite and infinite, the ephemeral and eternal.

Man needs material things and spiritual values. He has basic needs of food and shelter. I am familiar with impoverished Indian people. They never lose their dignity even in poverty. They are honest and wise people. However, their daily struggle is to fulfill the basic needs of food. "To them, God can only appear as bread and butter." Gandhi said. You are more willing to embrace the essential, spiritual values when you do not need to worry about the material things. If your stomach is empty, you can't be interested in metaphysics. When the basic needs are fulfilled, your mind is more open to achieve higher significance in life.

Therefore, money is needed. Money is one of the greatest inventions of man. The barter system was complicated in the past. The creation of money made the exchange simple. Money is a necessary and useful means. The problem arises when money becomes the end. You should always remain the master of your money. Life is empty when you fill it only with the visible and forget that the essential is invisible. Your life is rich when you have something beyond the trade. Unless you have something which is not material, you can't have a meaningful life.

Journey Into Your Inner World

Money Is Not All There Is

We are born rich. In India, a little boy is nicknamed *raja* (king) and a little girl *rani* (queen). All children in their birth are kings and queens. Their attitude is royal and grandiose. They are godlike. An emperor or a beggar is the same to their eyes. They are playful and joyful. They are living their lives fully. What happens to these kings and queens when they grow up?

As they are growing, they lose their innocent joy that made them happy when they saw a little bird or caressed a rabbit. They become serious about gaining material things. But only your body can be satisfied by material things. Your soul can only be satisfied by the Infinite. With money, you can buy almost everything you want. But unless you know something which cannot be sold or be purchased by money, you will miss what is essential. The masters have a treasure of spiritual values that they would share with others but their nuggets of wisdom can never be purchased or sold.

Man has spiritual needs. Money cannot purchase the spiritual values of love, compassion, and peace of mind. These few things might be exceptions, but they do not have any price.

Society measures someone by what they have. The *Vedanta* (a Hindu philosophy) tells us that the greatness of a person is not measured by what he does or has, but by what he *is*. You know how to have more. To learn how to be more, one has to look inwardly and first become rich inside themselves. Buddha says, "Just as a candle cannot burn without fire, men cannot live without a spiritual life." The realization of spirituality is within. Take a journey into your inner world and live a more spiritual life.

Enter Your Inner World More Often

You have to come back home in order to experience a spiritual life. You are used to living in the outside world. You never think of another world which is inside you. You need to change your attitude to live a spiritual life. The attitude toward the outside world and the inner world is not the same.

The Attitude of the Masters *by Céline Théron*

In the outside world, you are not alone. The inner world is the depths of your being. You have to leave the crowd far behind. You should retire into solitude, alone, without companions. When you are utterly alone, the greatest spiritual experiences can happen. The masters are solitary sages who take their inner journey to practice the highest spiritual life.

It is hard to reach our own spiritual excellence because our title, position and status follow us everywhere, even at home. That personality is good when you are dealing with other people. It is a barrier when you start dealing with yourself. You have to leave outside of you whatever hinders your inner journey.

It is reported that Queen Victoria went to see her husband Prince Albert after an argument. The door of his room was closed. She knocked on the door.

Albert asked, "Who's there?" Victoria said, "The Queen of England." Albert did not respond. Victoria knocked on the door again.

Albert asked, "Who's there?" Victoria replied, "The Queen of England." The door remained closed. Victoria knocked for the third time.

"Who's there?" Albert asked yet again. "Your wife, Albert." the Queen replied. Her husband immediately opened the door.

Whether this story is historical or not, it shows that you cannot use your worldly status at home. Queen Victoria loved her husband. But her status as a queen made her husband reluctant to open the door. Likewise, if you want the door of spirituality to open, you have to leave outside your status. You have to embark on your spiritual journey alone. You do not need to always keep your worldly life separate from your spiritual life. You can turn your daily life into an ecstasy moment, however.

Transform Your Worldly Life

It is not often possible to mark the difference between a worldly experience and a spiritual experience, or a divine one. When a child is smiling at you, can you say what is spiritual and what is not? Man and the divine are mingled together on earth. God takes different appearances. At one moment, he is in the milk that the mother feeds her child, in a loving woman the next. He can be in the song of the cuckoo or in the fragrance of a flower. In a carved statue, you can see a stone or a divinity. The man who can recognize Him in all his disguises is realizing a divine experience.

When you feel love for living human beings who surround you, for all living beings and everything that is visible, then you can see the invisible. Love is the bridge on which you can walk to reach divinity. Love is the greatest spiritual value there is. The moment love touches anything, it transforms it from the lower into the higher, from the common into the poetic, from the worldly into the spiritual.

Love should first begin at home.

I loved the peasants' houses in my neighbourhood. Their houses contained everything needful. They reminded me how, in reality, so few are the true necessities of man.

When you entered a peasant's house, on the left were two stones that served for cooking. The house was illuminated by the fire coming from the dried cow-dung patties used as a fuel for cooking. The earthenware pots and jars lined in a corner next to a pitcher of fresh water. On the wall, deity icons were hanging and a rolled mat was leaning. In a hole in the wall, an earthen lamp candle was burning. An odor of incense hung in the air. The *saree* transformed into a stand-by cradle was attached on wood poles holding the roof up. Behind the house, in the tiny garden, there was a sheep. Under a papaya tree laden with fruits, fowls were picking grains. And inside the house, a mother swung her child's cradle to help her little one sleep.

Peasant houses may appear empty, but the peasants who dwell in them live a peaceful life. Simple things such as eating have a meaning for them. In fact, eating for them was a great moment.

The Attitude of the Masters *by Céline Théron*

Speaking of food, we have developed a wrong attitude towards it. It is viewed simply as a pleasure we can grow fat on.

I remember eating as a spiritual moment. In my country, when the children cry or refuse to eat, the mothers would show them the moon. When I was a little girl, Mama gave me food on the balcony of our home so that I could see the moon. The moon made us cool and calm. While eating in the presence of the moon, the food nourished not only the body but also the spirit. An Indian woman has been taught to think of her husband as a god. Mama was a traditional Indian woman. She had a devotional attitude toward her husband. Mama added something sacred in her daily cooking. She served food to my dad with great care. She never ate before him.

Mother was an ordinary housewife, busy all day long with her work, but she did everything with *bakthi* (devotion). She used to get up before sunrise to present her daily tribute to the new day. Her first job was the sweeping of the courtyard, which was sprinkled with a mixture of cow dung and water to lay the dust and keep it fresh and clean. While her hands were occupied with this task, her lips would be singing the name of the Lord. This sweet sound filled the morning air with purity. Then she would draw a beautiful *kolum* (design) with rice powder in our house entrance. She followed this tradition of using the rice powder to invite birds and other small creatures like ants to eat it. Thus, Mama was welcoming other beings into our home.

Through this sign of invitation to welcome all into the home Mama was teaching me some of the deepest wisdom: harmonious coexistence of all beings. She showed me how a simple act can hold a profound spiritual meaning.

You can transform your worldly life into a spiritual experience. When you prepare food for your beloved, make it a spiritual experience. When you embrace him or her, feel the quietude arising in you. When your child returns home from school, admire him as you would admire a beautiful dove flying to you. When a friend visits you, receive him with a blissful state of mind. That is the attitude of the masters who live their daily lives as moments of ecstasy. You live broadly and fully when your transform simple attitudes into spiritual ones.

Be Aware Of Your Divine Nature

Remember that divinity is the true nature of Man. When you see god in others, you have a completely different attitude toward life. Little by little, everything around you, without changing shape, has a spiritual value to it.

To reach your greatest level of spiritual experience, you have to always rise higher. You are god-like; you are gods. Do not cast off your divinity and settle for less than that. Do not view life like a raven that looks to see whether or not a crumb is left over. Life gives you a great challenge to be more than you are. The lion has no other evolution than to be a lion whereas man can choose his attitude. He can fall to the level of an animal or rise high to the level of divinity.

A lotus leaf grows in water but it is never moistened by it. So a man should live in this world like a lotus leaf, his feet standing on the earth and his soul melting with the divine. You carry the truth of divinity in your soul. It kicks within like a child when the time has come for it to leave the womb of its mother. One more step, and you are aware of your divine nature. The masters who unfolded their divine nature knew that secret behind transformation. They had the greatest skill in the world to make god out of man. The divine nature is within oneself and it is not to be sought outside. Daily life has led you astray, so you did not get the chance to let your divinity flower within you. Change your attitude to allow the ultimate spiritual growth to happen in you.

In Mahabalipuram, an historic town in India, you can see ancient monuments built by the Pallava Kings, among them the king Narsimha. I have seen in Mahabalipuram the artist carving deity statues. He meticulously works on the stone, transforming it little by little. The sculptor goes on hammering, cutting away unnecessary pieces, throwing away all that is

The Attitude of the Masters *by Céline Théron*

inessential. Then, by and by, the image of the deity is discovered. When the inessential is cut away and the essential is revealed, then divinity comes out in its total glory. The sculptor makes god out of stone. Before the artist used the chisel and hammer on the stone, the divinity was there but hidden by the inessential pieces.

Similarly, you have to work on yourself to bring out your divinity. The inessential has to be broken and thrown away so that the essential comes up. When your thoughts and attitudes become noble, the infinite god behind those noble thoughts and attitudes manifests itself more and more. When you get rid of the inessential that hinders your spiritual growth, then the divinity inside will appear. You are simply changing, transforming into the divine. And you can reach your divine nature through your attitude.

CHAPTER TEN

Sharing Makes the World Better

Sharing Makes the World Better

I once saw a beggar in a French countryside marketplace. He was always sitting on the corner of the street reaching out with his hand toward all who passed by. It was a busy marketplace. People were always in a hurry. Rarely, a walker halted before the beggar to give him a coin. One day, a man opened his purse and put a coin on the beggar's empty hand. The beggar looked at the coin with a frowning brow and an angry gleam in his eyes. He then threw away the coin and yelled at the man, "You give me twenty cents? Keep it yourself!" Meanwhile, a crowd had gathered to watch this scene unfold. The man felt so humiliated that he blushed and walked away with his head down.

Receive with an Open Heart

For someone who knows how to receive anything with an open heart, twenty cents can be valuable. Here the master Krishna is a great example. I am reminded of one of his stories. Sudama, a childhood friend of Krishna, was a poor Brahmin. His wife once persuaded him to meet Krishna, who was now the ruler of Dwarka and who could relieve them of their poverty. Sudama visited Krishna with an offering of parched rice as he could afford nothing else. Krishna sensed the feeling of love behind this offering and gave him countless riches. Krishna had the attitude of the master.

The masters know how to receive even a simple gift with an open heart.

But the beggar of the marketplace rejected the coin, and by so doing he hurt the feelings of the man who had given it to him. Finally, the beggar had refused a most generous act: to receive.

Yes, receiving is also a generosity. We often talk about the generosity of giving, but receiving is a generous act too. We want to be a giver. We do not want to be a receiver. You are joyful when you give. Make others happy by allowing them to give something to you. To give love is a great attitude. But how many people on earth are suffering because there is no one to receive their love? When a person accepts your love, it is a generous attitude they displayed towards you. She was receptive. She allowed you to melt your heart into her being.

Receive with an open heart, but do not be only a receiver. Some people's constant attitude is to only receive. They live their life in the name of getting things. They are always waiting for something from others, but they will not give anything back. They have never tasted the joy of giving. Life is giving and receiving. The attitude of giving and receiving can change the world.

Change the World in Your Own Way

We all have the power to change the world. With the right attitude and a burning compassion, you can make a huge difference in the world. When I say the world, I'm talking about your world. Yes, start first with the world around you. It is like a forest fire. If you make a significant difference in the lives of the people around you, it will spread.

Sharing Makes the World Better

In my private school in India, the majority of the children belonged to rich families. A minority were poor. The wealthy children stayed away from the poor children. During recreation, they ate costly biscuits. They drank *Horlicks* (a malted milk made with hot milk.) The children from poor families who had had no breakfast before coming to school looked with sad eyes at the rich kids who had biscuits and *Horlicks* to eat and drink.

During school festival, grand amusements were organized. Only those who had money could participate in the games. A merchant came every year during this school event with many different fancy things. He spread a mat. He displayed all kinds of jewelry: earrings, clips, and bracelets. Fortunate little girls bought whatever they liked whereas penniless girls watched them with frustration. Some mischievous kids would go as far as to mock them by pointing out their poverty.

I was fortunate to buy whatever I liked. As a child, I was very selfish. I did not want to share. I hid my color pens and snack to avoid sharing them with other kids.

But it is never too late to change our attitude; we can become more open to the needs of other people. Sharing makes this world a better place. When we want to keep everything for ourselves, we cannot create a better world. Your life is rich when you make somebody else's life rich. The masters are always givers.

Give like the Wellspring

Normal economics tells you that the more you give the less you will have, and that your coffer will be empty if you go on giving. People will tell you stories about rich men ruined because of their charitable attitude who were now begging at the gate of the temple. However, the masters know that the more you give, the more you will receive. The economy of sharing has a different rule.

You have a truly rich life when you know that giving is receiving. The well that gives away its water is continuously replenished with fresh water. It is never exhausted. The wellspring with water that is untouched begins to stink. Then its source slowly dries up. The person who does not want to share and becomes stingy is like a dried up well. Be like the wellspring that goes on increasing its water by quenching people's thirst. You should never give by force or in pain. Be delighted when you give. That joy is your reward. If you are not a giver today, you can become one tomorrow.

Be the Giver You Want Your Children to Be
You can encourage your kids to share through your own attitude of caring and sharing. You will give them a good example to follow as a result. The seeds of generosity that my parents planted in my childhood sprouted later. I learned the generosity through my parents' attitude toward impoverished people.

Mama was a very sensitive woman. If a beggar came to our door Mother would never allow him or her to go away empty-handed. She saw a beggar as God in human form. If any poor people were there at our meal time, Mama would say, "We must first give, and afterwards we can eat." This teaching of hers made such an impression on me. She gave me so much else, milk to drink, food to eat, and stayed awake late at night to care for me when I was sick; but this teaching was the greatest gift of all she offered to me.

Sharing Makes the World Better

This picture of my mother always reminds me of her generous spirit. Mother taught me some of the deepest truths of philosophy, but she made it into a little poem: Giving is Godlike. That was her lasting gift to me.

The Attitude of the Masters *by Céline Théron*

From all my treasured memories of Mother this story is a precious one. One day, a woman who was a beggar clothed in shabby *saree* was at the doorway of our house asking for food. The old woman's hair was matted and filthy. She had a strong bad smell clinging to her. She probably had not bathed in years. Her *saree* was sticking to her body. Mama invited her into our garden fountain. Even if we had maids, Mama did everything herself. She filled up many pitchers with water. She gave a bath to the old lady. She helped her by giving her a new *saree*.

She offered delicious food to the lady, served in a traditional way. The lady sat down on a mat. Mama spread a banana leaf in front of the guest. She first served plain rice accompanied with a savory *kootu* (mixed vegetables with grated coconut), added *sambar* (a vegetable stew.) The old lady started eating with her bony hand with a sprinkling of ghee. Meanwhile, for the dessert Mama brought from our kitchen *paayasam* (sweet milk pudding.) Once the old lady finished the meal, Mama gave her a betel leaf and betel nut which can aid in digestion. It is also a sign of hospitality.

Before the lady left, Mama gave her a rupee. The old woman eyes were soaked with tears. She clasped my mother's hands between her own. "Thank you, my daughter!" she said as she squeezed Mama's hands affectionately.

Mama also used to prepare *kanji* (rice boiled in a large amount of water until it softens significantly.) She set upon the veranda of our house an earthenware pot of poured *kanji*. On a banana leaf, she spread spicy mango pickle, chili and shallot. People passing by served themselves and took a rest in the shadow of the veranda.

My dad was also a very generous man. He always helped others without being asked to. He went on giving to relatives and friends. He rose up many strangers from poverty to a good position.

One afternoon, he returned home in his undergarments. On his way to home, he had met an acquaintance who urgently needed proper dress for an important appointment. So dad gave him the costly shirt and pants that he was wearing. But when my dad was in a difficult time, there was nobody to help him.

We often expect gratitude from people for the favour we did to them. Gratitude is a rare flower that blooms in one's heart. Share, and forget your generosity. Give without asking gratitude in response. On the contrary, you should feel grateful to have the opportunity to give, and that your gift has not been refused. The real giver through us is *life*. Be like a fruit tree. It gives fruits to everybody without deciding who deserves it and who does not, but it has never tasted its own fruits. Sometimes you cannot taste the sweetness of your generosity in return. The attitude of the masters is to give without expecting any return. Every giving has to be unconditional. Then giving leads you close to the divine.

Giving is an Attitude

A certain great king went to hunt in a forest. He happened to meet a sage. The king felt delighted after having a conversation with the sage. He became so pleased that he told the sage, "*Swami* (spiritual master), I'd like to offer you a present." The sage said, "I am perfectly satisfied with what I have." The king insisted, "Just to purify me, come with me into the city and take the present."

At last, the sage consented to go to the king. He was taken into the king's palace. Wealth and power were manifest everywhere. The king asked the sage to wait for a moment while he went to a corner and began to pray, "Lord, give me more wealth, more children, more territory." Meanwhile, the sage got up and began to walk away.

The king saw him going and went after him. "Stay, *Swami*; you are going away before taking my present."

The sage turned to him and said, "Beggar, I do not beg from beggars. What can you give? You have been begging yourself all the time."

The Attitude of the Masters *by Céline Théron*

Giving is an attitude. You can have the inexhaustible wealth of an emperor, yet have an attitude of a beggar. Once, a man asked a beggar, "What will you do if you became rich?" The beggar replied, "I will beg with a golden begging bowl." The beggar does not want to give up his attitude of a beggar even though his status would change. You are an emperor, not a beggar. Adopt the attitude of a master and the attitude of a giver.

The attitude of giving is much more important than what you give. Buddha and his disciple Ananda were going from house to house to beg food. A child was playing with sand. She ran to Buddha and said, "You can eat this too." Then, she put into his bowl a handful of earth. Ananda was about to yell at the kid. Buddha told Ananda, "Do not look at what this child put in my bowl but think about her intention. She wanted to give me something to eat. So, she gave what she had in her hands. The kid gave from her kindness. Thus, I am very happy." The heart of giving is the root of the giver, no matter what you give.

Giving does not always mean giving materials goods. You can give a smile. You can give a kind word. Leo Tolstoy, as he walked down the street, passed by a beggar. Tolstoy pulled out of his pocket a dilapidated leather purse. He found that his purse was empty. Looking at the poor man, Tolstoy said, "I'm sorry, my brother. I have no money to give." The beggar brightened, and a smile lit up his face. He said with a radiant expression, "Don't worry, brother. You have given me a gift. You called me brother." What did Tolstoy truly give to the man? He respected the man as a man, not as a beggar. That is the attitude of a great man who makes every man great.

What you give of yourself means much more than just giving out material things. I once met four very young kids in front of a restaurant in India. They were dressed in rags, barefoot, holding one another by the hand, and begging. They were three girls and a boy. The eldest of them looked about eight years old. The youngest was still a baby. The eldest girl was carrying her little brother in her arms. She was kissing and caressing him so that he wouldn't cry. I bought them food, toys and dresses. I also talked with the eldest girl about her life. She said, "Mama is ill. Dad is always drinking. He rarely comes home." At her age, she should be in school and play like other children; instead, she was carrying the burden of the whole family. She gave herself for the love for her sisters and brother.

The masters who have given themselves to lighten the burden of man and gave hope to humanity have transformed the world for the better. They became immortal.

The Unquenchable Desire for Immortality

An unquenchable desire for immortality is part of human nature. Man longs to leave an indelible trace behind him. You have probably seen on trees the symbol of two hearts pierced by spear and names engraved on mountains. People had left their mark on things that last throughout the earth. If we can give life to those inscriptions, it would say a lot about how mankind yearns to be remembered forever. Many people have a desire to somehow to make their name immortal. Poets, painters or writers have tried to become immortal through their creations. Some, by attaining the peak of success and celebrity, wanted to leave their names burned on brass forever.

We all believe that we are the center of the cosmos. Look at the reality behind that fallacy. Millions of people are passing away every day without anyone noticing them. Many famous people have lived on this earth. Who remembers all their names? Even if thousands of people still remember the celebrities of golden times, it would not give life to them again.

Some people are still alive because of their attitude of masters. They live forever like Buddha, Sri Ramakrishna and Mahatma Gandhi. They realized great spiritual values such as truth, love and compassion. Their faith in their missions carried nations with them.

The Attitude of the Masters *by Céline Théron*

People have a different ultimate purpose in life. Some people live to die, and others die to live. There are people whose aim is to enjoy their lives as much as possible. Some others are not concerned for their lives. They feel that all men are one. They lighten the misery of man by their noble deeds. Finally, few people are the flower of humanity, a flower that never withers. They are the masters of the universe. They feel one with the entire universe, human, animals, vegetables, and minerals. They transform the ephemeral life on this earth into eternity. Buddha raises his hand. He touches the earth and says, "The earth is my witness!" The earth is the witness that they are immortal. Their deepest *karuna* (compassion) transforms the world. Their attitude on the earth makes them immortal. They become a legend.

Leave Your Personal Legend

The legend is not only for kings, historical leaders or great personalities. Every one of us has a legend. Ask yourself the question, "Who am I?" Without possessions, success, and fame, who are you? Your answer is your legacy.

Your attitude has the power to create your legend.

Once upon a time, an Englishman in India went down the street riding on his bike. He saw a crowd in a panic.

He asked them, "What has happened?"

"A man has fallen into the river" they replied.

The Englishman removed his clothes and jumped into the water to save the man who had fallen. When he came out of the water, both his clothes and his bike had been stolen.

The Englishman said, "Today, I did two good things. I saved a life, and I helped a poor Indian with my clothes and my bike."

Here I am telling the story of a man who was not a CEO of a big company, or an internationally renowned artist or a celebrity. He was a stranger, an unknown person. I tell you his story because of the difference he made in the life of someone else. His story is written in a book because of his noble attitude. This attitude changes an ordinary person into an extraordinary one.

You don't need a title to act as a master. While the crowd did nothing to save the man who had fallen into the river, the Englishman took action. That is the attitude of the master who has the ability to stand out from the crowd. Moreover, he served an immortal value: compassion. He left his legend by his courageous and compassionate attitude.

There is a higher power than man in the universe. By serving this higher power, man reaches his highest purpose. You create your legend by serving something immortal such as: love. Love has the quality of something beyond this world. Love is divine.

Remember that two days are important in life. The day you are born and the day you proved to yourself why you were born. People who have proved to themselves why they were born were at the service of something immortal. What immortal values can you serve during your life? The masters always stand for an immortal value. Your attitude as a master is your legend.

Epilogue

Congratulations! You did it! You read the book all the way to the end. Statistics tell us that only a handful of people read books from cover to cover. You are obviously one of the elite few.

Now that you finished reading *The Attitude of the Masters*, you have two choices. First, you can make it a fundamental part of your being or you can do nothing and find yourself stuck in neutral. I encourage you to choose the first option.

Also, I highly encourage you to exemplify *The Attitude of the Masters*. Work on yourself day and night to apply the lessons you learned. You should also share them with those in your surroundings.

Gandhi said, "We need to be the change we wish to see in the world." You can open up possibilities and create incredible breakthroughs for others with your attitude. You can reach new heights and achieve more by consistently showing up with the attitude of a master.

I wish you a life filled with joy and excitement. And finally, please make sure you share with me how you are applying what you've learned.

Resources to Help You Embrace The Attitude of the Masters

If you have been inspired by *The Attitude of the Masters* wisdom in this book and want to learn more, coaching and mentoring programs, as well as seminars are available at CelineTheron.com.

Details on booking Céline Théron for *The Attitude of the Masters'* presentation for your organization are also here:

www.CelineTheron.com
Phone: +33 (0)1 83 94 84 62
Email: Celine@CelineTheron.com

www.ingramcontent.com/pod-product-compliance
Lightning Source LLC
Chambersburg PA
CBHW022304060426
42446CB00007BA/482